Get Ready!

FOR STANDARDIZED TESTS

GRADE TWO

Other Books in the *Get Ready!* Series:

Get Ready! for Standardized Tests: Grade 1 by Joseph Harris, Ph.D.

Get Ready! for Standardized Tests: Grade 3 by Karen Mersky, Ph.D.

Get Ready! for Standardized Tests: Grade 4 by Joseph Harris, Ph.D.

Get Ready! for Standardized Tests: Grade 5 by Leslie E. Talbott, Ph.D.

Get Ready! for Standardized Tests: Grade 6 by Shirley Vickery, Ph.D.

TEST PREPARATION SERIES

Get Ready!

FOR STANDARDIZED TESTS

GRADE TWO

Joseph Harris, Ph.D.

Carol Turkington
Series Editor

McGraw-Hill

New York   San Francisco   Washington, D.C.   Auckland   Bogotá
Caracas   Lisbon   London   Madrid   Mexico City   Milan
Montreal   New Delhi   San Juan   Singapore
Sydney   Tokyo   Toronto

Library of Congress Cataloging-in-Publication Data

Get ready! for standardized tests / c Carol Turkington, series editor.
   p. cm.
   Includes bibliographical references.
   Contents: [1] Grade 1 / Joseph Harris — [2] Grade 2 / Joseph Harris — [3] Grade 3 / Karen Mersky — [4] Grade 4 / Joseph Harris — [5] Grade 5 / Leslie E. Talbott — [6] Grade 6 / Shirley Vickery.
   ISBN 0-07-136010-7 (v. 1) — ISBN 0-07-136011-5 (v. 2) — ISBN 0-07-136012-3 (v. 3) — ISBN 0-07-136013-1 (v. 4) — ISBN 0-07-136014-X (v. 5) — ISBN 0-07-136015-8 (v. 6)
   1. Achievement tests—United States—Study guides.   2. Education, Elementary—United States—Evaluation.   3. Education, Elementary—Parent participation—United States.   I. Turkington, Carol.   II. Harris, Joseph.

LB3060.22 .G48   2000
372.126—dc21   00-056083

McGraw-Hill

A Division of The McGraw·Hill Companies

1 2 3 4 5 6 7 8 9 0 PBT/PBT 0 9 8 7 6 5 4 3 2 1 0

ISBN 0-07-136011-5

This book was set in New Century Schoolbook by Inkwell Publishing Services.

Printed and bound by Phoenix Book Technology.

McGraw-Hill books are available at special quantity discounts to use as premiums and sales promotions, or for use in corporate training programs. For more information, please write to the Director of Special Sales, McGraw-Hill, Professional Publishing, Two Penn Plaza, New York, NY 10121-2298. Or contact your local bookstore.

To my son, Ross Adam Harris

Contents

SKILLS CHECKLIST

MY CHILD …	HAS LEARNED	IS WORKING ON
WORD ANALYSIS		
Initial consonant sounds		
Final consonant sounds		
Vowel sounds		
Word recognition		
Word study		
Contractions		
Root words		
Suffixes		
VOCABULARY		
Picture vocabulary		
Synonyms		
Antonyms		
Multiple-meaning words		
READING COMPREHENSION		
Picture comprehension		
Critical reading		
Story comprehension		
Giving a title		
LANGUAGE EXPRESSION		
Plurals		
Possession		
Pronouns		
Verb forms		
Adjectives		
Double negatives		
Paragraphs		
LANGUAGE MECHANICS		
Capitalization		
Punctuation		
MATH CONCEPTS		
Recognizing 0 to 100		
Numbers over 100		
Comparing and ordering numbers		
Number sentences		
Fraction parts		
Ordinal position		
Rounding and estimating		
Counting by 10s		
Skip counting		
Place value		
Number line		
Terminology		
MATH COMPUTATION		
Addition		
Subtraction		
Multiplication		
Division		
MATH APPLICATIONS		
Perimeters		
Matching shapes		
Plane and solid figures		
Spatial relations		
Estimating		
Standard units of measure		
Metric units of measure		
Word problems		
Time		
Calendars		
Money		

Introduction

Almost all of us have taken standardized tests in school. We spent several days bubbling-in answers, shifting in our seats. No one ever told us why we took the tests or what they would do with the results. We just took them and never heard about them again.

Today many parents aren't aware they are entitled to see their children's permanent records and, at a reasonable cost, to obtain copies of any information not protected by copyright, including testing scores. Late in the school year, most parents receive standardized test results with confusing bar charts and detailed explanations of scores that few people seem to understand.

In response to a series of negative reports on the state of education in this country, Americans have begun to demand that something be done to improve our schools. We have come to expect higher levels of accountability as schools face the competing pressures of rising educational expectations and declining school budgets. High-stakes standardized tests are rapidly becoming the main tool of accountability for students, teachers, and school administrators. If students' test scores don't continually rise, teachers and principals face the potential loss of school funding and, ultimately, their jobs. Summer school and private after-school tutorial program enrollments are swelling with students who have not met score standards or who, everyone agrees, could score higher.

While there is a great deal of controversy about whether it is appropriate for schools to use standardized tests to make major decisions about individual students, it appears likely that standardized tests are here to stay. They will be used to evaluate students, teachers, and the schools; schools are sure to continue to use students' test scores to demonstrate their accountability to the community.

The purposes of this guide are to acquaint you with the types of standardized tests your children may take; to help you understand the test results; and to help you work with your children in skill areas that are measured by standardized tests so they can perform as well as possible.

Types of Standardized Tests

The two major types of group standardized tests are *criterion-referenced tests* and *norm-referenced tests*. Think back to when you learned to tie your shoes. First Mom or Dad showed you how to loosen the laces on your shoe so that you could insert your foot; then they showed you how to tighten the laces—but not too tight. They showed you how to make bows and how to tie a knot. All the steps we just described constitute what is called a *skills hierarchy:* a list of skills from easiest to most difficult that are related to some goal, such as tying a shoelace.

Criterion-referenced tests are designed to determine at what level students are performing on various skills hierarchies. These tests assume that development of skills follows a sequence of steps. For example, if you were teaching shoelace tying, the skills hierarchy might appear this way:

1. Loosen laces.
2. Insert foot.
3. Tighten laces.
4. Make loops with both lace ends.
5. Tie a square knot.

Criterion-referenced tests try to identify how far along the skills hierarchy the student has progressed. There is no comparison against anyone else's score, only against an expected skill level. The main question criterion-referenced tests ask is: "Where is this child in the development of this group of skills?"

Norm-referenced tests, in contrast, are typically constructed to compare children in their abilities as to different skills areas. Although the experts who design test items may be aware of skills hierarchies, they are more concerned with how much of some skill the child has mastered, rather than at what level on the skills hierarchy the child is.

Ideally, the questions on these tests range from very easy items to those that are impossibly difficult. The essential feature of norm-referenced tests is that scores on these measures can be compared to scores of children in similar groups. They answer this question: "How does the child compare with other children of the same age or grade placement in the development of this skill?"

This book provides strategies for increasing your child's scores on both standardized norm-referenced and criterion-referenced tests.

The Major Standardized Tests

Many criterion-referenced tests currently in use are created locally or (at best) on a state level,

and there are far too many of them to go into detail here about specific tests. However, children prepare for them in basically the same way they do for norm-referenced tests.

A very small pool of norm-referenced tests is used throughout the country, consisting primarily of the Big Five:

- California Achievement Tests (CTB/McGraw-Hill)
- Iowa Tests of Basic Skills (Riverside)
- Metropolitan Achievement Test (Harcourt-Brace & Company)
- Stanford Achievement Test (Psychological Corporation)
- TerraNova [formerly Comprehensive Test of Basic Skills] (McGraw-Hill)

These tests use various terms for the academic skills areas they assess, but they generally test several types of reading, language, and mathematics skills, along with social studies and science. They may include additional assessments, such as of study and reference skills.

How States Use Standardized Tests

Despite widespread belief and practice to the contrary, group standardized tests are designed to assess and compare the achievement of groups. They are *not* designed to provide detailed diagnostic assessments of individual students. (For detailed individual assessments, children should be given individual diagnostic tests by properly qualified professionals, including trained guidance counselors, speech and language therapists, and school psychologists.) Here are examples of the types of questions group standardized tests are designed to answer:

- How did the reading achievement of students at Valley Elementary School this year compare with their reading achievement last year?

- How did math scores at Wonderland Middle School compare with those of students at Parkside Middle School this year?

- As a group, how did Hilltop High School students compare with the national averages in the achievement areas tested?

- How did the district's first graders' math scores compare with the district's fifth graders' math scores?

The fact that these tests are designed primarily to test and compare groups doesn't mean that test data on individual students isn't useful. It does mean that when we use these tests to diagnose individual students, we are using them for a purpose for which they were not designed.

Think of group standardized tests as being similar to health fairs at the local mall. Rather than check into your local hospital and spend thousands of dollars on full, individual tests for a wide range of conditions, you can go from station to station and take part in different health screenings. Of course, one would never diagnose heart disease or cancer on the basis of the screening done at the mall. At most, suspicious results on the screening would suggest that you need to visit a doctor for a more complete examination.

In the same way, group standardized tests provide a way of screening the achievement of many students quickly. Although you shouldn't diagnose learning problems solely based on the results of these tests, the results can tell you that you should think about referring a child for a more definitive, individual assessment.

An individual student's group test data should be considered only a point of information. Teachers and school administrators may use standardized test results to support or question hypotheses they have made about students; but these scores must be used alongside other information, such as teacher comments, daily work, homework, class test grades, parent observations, medical needs, and social history.

Valid Uses of Standardized Test Scores

Here are examples of appropriate uses of test scores for individual students:

- Mr. Cone thinks that Samantha, a third grader, is struggling in math. He reviews her file and finds that her first- and second-grade standardized test math scores were very low. Her first- and second-grade teachers recall episodes in which Samantha cried because she couldn't understand certain math concepts, and mention that she was teased by other children, who called her "Dummy." Mr. Cone decides to refer Samantha to the school assistance team to determine whether she should be referred for individual testing for a learning disability related to math.

- The local college wants to set up a tutoring program for elementary school children who are struggling academically. In deciding which youngsters to nominate for the program, the teachers consider the students' averages in different subjects, the degree to which students seem to be struggling, parents' reports, and standardized test scores.

- For the second year in a row, Gene has performed poorly on the latest round of standardized tests. His teachers all agree that Gene seems to have some serious learning problems. They had hoped that Gene was immature for his class and that he would do better this year; but his dismal grades continue. Gene is referred to the school assistance team to determine whether he should be sent to the school psychologist for assessment of a possible learning handicap.

Inappropriate Use of Standardized Test Scores

Here are examples of how schools have sometimes used standardized test results inappropriately:

- Mr. Johnson groups his students into reading groups solely on the basis of their standardized test scores.

- Ms. Henry recommends that Susie be held back a year because she performed poorly on the standardized tests, despite strong grades on daily assignments, homework, and class tests.

- Gerald's teacher refers him for consideration in the district's gifted program, which accepts students using a combination of intelligence test scores, achievement test scores, and teacher recommendations. Gerald's intelligence test scores were very high. Unfortunately, he had a bad cold during the week of the standardized group achievement tests and was taking powerful antihistamines, which made him feel sleepy. As a result, he scored too low on the achievement tests to qualify.

The public has come to demand increasingly high levels of accountability for public schools. We demand that schools test so that we have hard data with which to hold the schools accountable. But too often, politicians and the public place more faith in the test results than is justified. Regardless of whether it's appropriate to do so and regardless of the reasons schools use standardized test results as they do, many schools base crucial programming and eligibility decisions on scores from group standardized tests. It's to your child's advantage, then, to perform as well as possible on these tests.

Two Basic Assumptions

The strategies we present in this book come from two basic assumptions:

1. Most students can raise their standardized test scores.

2. Parents can help their children become stronger in the skills the tests assess.

This book provides the information you need

to learn what skill areas the tests measure, what general skills your child is being taught in a particular grade, how to prepare your child to take the tests, and what to do with the results. In the appendices you will find information to help you decipher test interpretations; a listing of which states currently require what tests; and additional resources to help you help your child to do better in school and to prepare for the tests.

A Word about Coaching

This guide is *not* about coaching your child. When we use the term *coaching* in referring to standardized testing, we mean trying to give someone an unfair advantage, either by revealing beforehand what exact items will be on the test or by teaching "tricks" that will supposedly allow a student to take advantage of some detail in how the tests are constructed.

Some people try to coach students in shrewd test-taking strategies that take advantage of how the tests are supposedly constructed rather than strengthening the students' skills in the areas tested. Over the years, for example, many rumors have been floated about "secret formulas" that test companies use.

This type of coaching emphasizes ways to help students obtain scores they didn't earn—to get something for nothing. Stories have appeared in the press about teachers who have coached their students on specific questions, parents who have tried to obtain advance copies of tests, and students who have written down test questions after taking standardized tests and sold them to others. Because of the importance of test security, test companies and states aggressively prosecute those who attempt to violate test security—and they should do so.

How to Raise Test Scores

Factors that are unrelated to how strong students are but that might artificially lower test scores include anything that prevents students from making scores that accurately describe their actual abilities. Some of those factors are:

- giving the tests in uncomfortably cold or hot rooms;

- allowing outside noises to interfere with test taking; and

- reproducing test booklets in such small print or with such faint ink that students can't read the questions.

Such problems require administrative attention from both the test publishers, who must make sure that they obtain their norms for the tests under the same conditions students face when they take the tests; and school administrators, who must ensure that conditions under which their students take the tests are as close as possible to those specified by the test publishers.

Individual students also face problems that can artificially lower their test scores, and parents can do something about many of these problems. Stomach aches, headaches, sleep deprivation, colds and flu, and emotional upsets due to a recent tragedy are problems that might call for the student to take the tests during make-up sessions. Some students have physical conditions such as muscle-control problems, palsies, or difficulty paying attention that require work over many months or even years before students can obtain accurate test scores on standardized tests. And, of course, some students just don't take the testing seriously or may even intentionally perform poorly. Parents can help their children overcome many of these obstacles to obtaining accurate scores.

Finally, with this book parents are able to help their children raise their scores by:

- increasing their familiarity (and their comfort level) with the types of questions on standardized tests;

- drills and practice exercises to increase their skill in handling the kinds of questions they will meet; and

- providing lots of fun ways for parents to help their children work on the skill areas that will be tested.

Test Questions

The favorite type of question for standardized tests is the multiple-choice question. For example:

1. The first President of the United States was:

   A Abraham Lincoln

   B Martin Luther King, Jr.

   C George Washington

   D Thomas Jefferson

The main advantage of multiple-choice questions is that it is easy to score them quickly and accurately. They lend themselves to optical scanning test forms, on which students fill in bubbles or squares and the forms are scored by machine. Increasingly, companies are moving from paper-based testing to computer-based testing, using multiple-choice questions.

The main disadvantage of multiple-choice questions is that they restrict test items to those that can be put in that form. Many educators and civil rights advocates have noted that the multiple-choice format only reveals a superficial understanding of the subject. It's not possible with multiple-choice questions to test a student's ability to construct a detailed, logical argument on some issue or to explain a detailed process. Although some of the major tests are beginning to incorporate more subjectively scored items, such as short answer or essay questions, the vast majority of test items continue to be in multiple-choice format.

In the past, some people believed there were special formulas or tricks to help test-takers determine which multiple-choice answer was the correct one. There may have been some truth to *some* claims for past tests. Computer analyses of some past tests revealed certain biases in how tests were constructed. For example, the old advice to pick *D* when in doubt appears to have been valid for some past tests. However, test publishers have become so sophisticated in their ability to detect patterns of bias in the formulation of test questions and answers that they now guard against it aggressively.

In Chapter 1, we provide information about general test-taking considerations, with advice on how parents can help students overcome testing obstacles. The rest of the book provides information to help parents help their children strengthen skills in the tested areas.

Joseph Harris, Ph.D.

Test-Taking Basics

Before we turn to specific strategies for taking tests, we need to understand the nature of the second-grade child. The brain structures necessary for learning to read, write, and perform mathematical calculations continue to develop during second grade.

Despite the great surge in development among most second graders, not all children progress at the same rate. Veteran second-grade teachers note that many children at this age are still simply immature. They will develop the ability to read, write, and calculate, but it will happen later on.

Physical Characteristics

By now almost all children are either left- or right-handed. Although some are still somewhat clumsy, most show much stronger balance and awareness of the body during movement. Expect your second grader to perform intricate fine-motor tasks, including writing, manipulating small objects, and even playing a musical instrument, all of which demand strong perceptual and motor skills.

How Second Graders Think

The late Swiss developmental psychologist Jean Piaget spent decades observing children at different ages, noting changes in their learning abilities. He provided a theory of children's thinking abilities that has had a major influence on Western education. According to Piaget's the-

ory, the typical second-grade child slowly begins to see the world from another's perspective and to become more logical. In addition, second graders begin to see the difference between animate and inanimate objects. They realize that items remain the same regardless of how we group them, so that a measuring cup full of peas is the same amount whether it's contained in the cup or spread out into a shallow dish.

Emotional and Behavioral Characteristics

Most second graders are much better than they were last year at sitting still and focusing on their schoolwork. Although they readily state that they don't enjoy some tasks, most understand they must sit still and pay attention.

With their budding logical skills, many second graders become preoccupied with issues of fairness. In fact, many second-grade teachers refer to "fair" as the "F Word" because they hear it so many times a day: It's not fair that Jack gets to walk at the front of the line; it's not fair that Kelli can't sit next to Lori; it's not fair that Josh has to do his math at home because he was playing in class.

Basic Test-Taking Strategies

Sometimes children score lower on standardized tests than their abilities warrant because they approach testing in an inefficient and unproductive manner. There are strategies that you can use before the test and that your child can use during testing to make sure that she does as well as possible.

Before the Test

Patience. Perhaps the most effective strategy in preparing your child for standardized tests is patience. Remember that no matter how much pressure we put on children, they won't learn skills until they are neurologically, physically, mentally, and emotionally ready to do so. There's a delicate balance between challenging your child to try a difficult task that he's ready for, and pressuring him to do something that is beyond his reach.

Parents of second graders see the progress their children make in second grade and become very ambitious for them. They buy software to teach their children advanced math or they demand that their children read books that are much too hard for second graders. It's good to challenge your child, but if you see that he isn't making progress or that he's getting frustrated, perhaps it is time to back off.

Be patient. Your child is at the beginning of a lifetime of learning. Normal children develop skills at different rates. As parents, we can't possibly be objective when it comes to own children. We may see a problem where none exists.

Talk with Your Child. Children at this age can have great insight into how they are doing in school. Your second grader may be able to tell you that he understands math but has trouble learning vocabulary words.

Remember too that problems with vision and hearing can surface at this age. Your child may tell you that he can't see the chalkboard or hear the teacher this year, although last year his vision and hearing were fine.

Talk with the Teacher. It's amazing how many frantic parents contact psychologists to have a child evaluated for learning disabilities or emotional disturbance because of problems they think the child *might* be having in school, without ever speaking with the teacher about their worries.

Don't wait for an invitation or for problems to develop before you meet your child's teacher. Get to know him as early in the school year as possible. If your schedule permits, volunteer to help with students during special programs or on field trips. Bring refreshments on party days. Help your child's teacher see you as an ally, someone she is comfortable contacting before small problems become big ones.

Most teachers are eager to keep you updated on your child's progress. They can give you materials and suggest activities for helping your child at home, and they can provide valuable perspective.

No Last-Minute Changes. Make as few changes as possible in your child's routine the day before and the morning of the test. If your child isn't used to going to bed at 8 p.m., putting him to bed early the night before the test will only frustrate him and may actually make it harder for him to get to sleep by the normal time. If an earlier bedtime is a good idea, make that change weeks before testing.

If your child skips breakfast or only eats buttered toast most mornings, serving him a hearty breakfast the day of the test will only make him feel heavy and sleepy. If your child is not eating a healthy breakfast, introduce better breakfast habits as far in advance as possible.

The most productive attitude you can take toward preparing your child for standardized tests is to prepare him to be a healthier and academically stronger student every day, not just on the day of the tests.

Neatness Counts. Finally, check to see how neatly your child can fill in the bubbles, squares, and rectangles in the figure on page 9. If he fills them in sloppily, overlaps the lines significantly, erases or pushes his pencil down with too much pressure, then you may want to have him practice the fine-motor activities that will help him fill in bubble sheets more neatly. For example, give him coloring books and connect-the-dots pages to work on those skills.

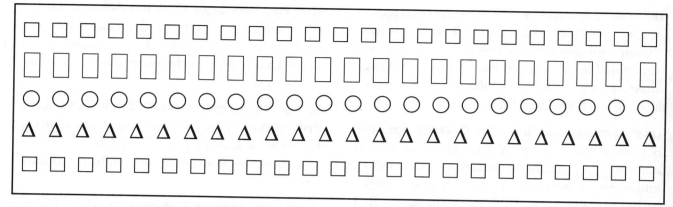

If you have a computer, you can easily create sheets of capital *O*s, squares, and rectangles that your child can practice filling in, or use the sample above.

During the Test

There are some strategies your child can use during standardized testing that have been shown to result in varying degrees of improvement in scores. Talk about the strategies below with your child and go over the list from time to time.

Bring Extra Pencils. Even if students are allowed to get up and sharpen pencils during the test, the very act of getting up, sharpening the pencils, and returning to their seats will use up precious test time. If your child breaks a pencil point or the pencil becomes dull and he only has to reach into his desk for another pencil, he'll have more time to work on test questions.

Listen Carefully. It's astounding how many mistakes children make simply because they do not listen to instructions or do not pay attention to demonstrations. During standardized testing, many children place checkmarks in bubbles or circle the bubbles instead of filling them in. Other children don't put their names on the test answer sheets, even though the teacher has specifically guided them through this step. Still others begin marking their answers on the wrong side of the form or go to the wrong section to begin marking.

Mark the Right Bubble. Make sure your child knows that he should always take care to mark the correct bubbles on the answer sheet. Convince your child that the machine used to scan the answer sheets won't be able to read minds, so he must be sure to mark the correct bubbles.

Read the Question First. Many children simply begin filling in bubbles without reading the entire question. The last few words in a question sometimes give the most important clues to the correct answer. Make sure your child reads the entire question before answering.

Read All Answer Choices First. Children tend to be impulsive. They may very well select the first plausible answer before reading a much better answer farther down the list. Again, tell your child not to hurry, and read all the answer possibilities first.

Skip Hard Items and Return Later. Many children, especially perfectionists, obsess over difficult test items. They may spend so much time on these problems that they never move on to others they would be able to answer correctly if they only had enough time left. Although some tests that involve listening don't lend themselves to saving difficult items for later, most do.

Refer to Pictures for Clues. Test publishers don't put random pictures in tests. Pictures may give valuable clues that children can combine with what they already know to find correct answers.

Don't Automatically Stick with the First Answer. One of the great myths in testing is that your first answer is always the right one. In reality, most of the time, when a student changes an answer, it's the right decision. It's also possible to improve your score by flagging answers you aren't sure about and returning later to work on them further.

Use Context to Find the Correct Answer. Students can frequently find clues to correct answers by looking at descriptions, wording, and other information in the questions themselves. For example, if the question states that Judy's father was frowning when he looked at the window and called Judy, that will provide a clue that perhaps Judy broke the window.

Infer Word Meaning from Context. When we run across unfamiliar words, most adults rarely stop and run to the dictionary to look them up. Instead, we look for meaning in the other parts of a sentence or paragraph that gives us clues to what meanings would be appropriate. Children can frequently figure out unfamiliar meanings from such clues.

Use Key Words to Find the Answer. Look at the questions and try to determine the parts that are important to solving the question and those that aren't. Verbs often hold very important clues.

Watch for Absolute Words Such as "Always" and "Never." Absolute words may be a clue that the answer using them is less likely to be correct, because some extreme condition must be true.

Eliminate Answer Choices. Sherlock Holmes was fond of saying, "Eliminate the impossible, and what remains is the truth." Children can narrow down their choices among multiple-choice items by eliminating answers they know can't possibly be true. This will allow them to focus on only the remaining answers.

In Chapter 2, we'll discuss how to help your child with word analysis skills, including word sounds, root words, and suffixes

Word Analysis

The 6-year-old who entered first grade last year able to say the alphabet and read a few words will probably begin second grade a reading veteran. Children in second grade can begin to enjoy the children's page in the Sunday newspaper, read children's magazines such as *Highlights for Children,* and even decipher the bills and ads that clog your mailbox!

What Your Second Grader Should Be Learning

Most second graders are able to understand fairly sophisticated written language. You'll be able to read to them from books on the same level that middle school students can read independently. You'll find your second grader following along with you as you read, often stopping you to point out new words. At the same time, her ability to recognize words will allow her to begin to read much more extensively. In fact, second grade is a time when many children begin to read independently.

Single-consonant sound recognition should be nearly flawless for most second graders, and middle to late second graders should have strong skills in identifying initial consonant blends, such as "pl," "sh," and "ch" sounds. Most, however, will continue to be confused by complicated consonant–vowel combinations, such as the "qu" combination in "quick" and "quiche." They are able to clearly identify ending consonant sounds. Middle and late second graders are

able to identify ending consonant blends, such as the "rt" in "start" and the "ng" in "long."

Most late second graders are familiar with the term "suffix" as well as its meaning, and understand compound words and root words.

What You and Your Child Can Do

The ability to understand and practice word analysis skills requires familiarity with a wide variety of words. Especially in English, in which many of our most important words are irregular, the more words we know the more readily we'll understand the rules and exceptions.

Read! One of the best ways to familiarize your child with words and the rules governing them is to read. Second graders are still young enough to appreciate and look forward to story time with mom or dad every day. By second grade, however, you'll see significant maturing in her tastes. You'll also find that your second grader will want to read to you during story time, although when reading out loud she'll need books at a younger reading level.

Encourage your child to read independently by following along with her and gently helping with words that cause problems. You'll have to experiment a little to determine how much prompting your child needs and how much she'll tolerate; but you have an advantage over the teacher because you can give your undivided attention. You can become an expert on your child's tastes, reading ability, and tolerance of correction. Point out interesting properties of words, such as the fact that *carp* and *kit* have the same beginning *k* sound, although they use different letters; or that *a* has one sound in *cat*, another in *age*, and yet another in *hall*.

Second graders are developing independent interests, and it shouldn't be too hard to find age-appropriate reading material on a wide variety of topics. Visit your second grader's classroom and note what books are on the shelves. Which ones are worn from use and which are untouched?

Take a trip to the local library with your child and make friends with the children's librarian. A children's librarian can be a real help in identifying age-appropriate materials. Even better, you can borrow books before buying them to determine which ones you want to buy.

Be a Resource. Encourage your second grader to come to you with words she doesn't know, or ask her to look them up in an age-appropriate dictionary. Many books designed for young readers have glossaries with most of the difficult words listed. Many books for this age now have definitions of new words in the margins. Encourage your child to make lists of new words. Review the lists with her from time to time, making sure that she can read and pronounce the words.

Communicate. Talk to your child. That advice may seem simplistic, but consider that the average father in the United States spends less than seven minutes a day with his children. Time spent together as a family around the supper table is becoming rare in today's fast-paced society; Jane is at soccer practice, Mom's working late, Tommy's at Scouts, and Dad eats alone in front of the TV.

Make time in your busy life for family members to talk and listen, which will help your child become more fluent with language. Hearing the spoken word will help her master rules for beginning, middle, and ending sounds, consonant blends, vowel sounds, and combination words. Point out "funny" words. When you're

with your child and you come across a word that you don't know, look up the word together.

Play Word Games. Playing word games is a great way to help children become familiar with word attack skills. See if you can crack the code for this game:

SUSIE: "Piano."

JANE: "Oregon."

ELLEN: "Never."

SUSIE: "Ravioli."

JANE: "Iron."

It's not hard: The first person says a word, and the next person must come up with a word beginning with the same sound as the ending sound in the word that came before. If the first word was "skate," the next person would say a word beginning with the "t" sound, not an "e" sound, because the "e" is silent. Anyone who can't come up with a word in 30 seconds has to drop out of the game. The last person remaining is the winner.

Word List. Ask your child's teacher for the state word list recommended for second graders. Most states now have such lists, and they can be a good way to find out what words your child will encounter in class and on standardized tests.

Create flash cards using these words, and play games with them. Note any problems your child may have with sounds, such as particular consonant blends or vowel combinations. Model the appropriate pronunciation.

Keep a Journal. Encourage your child to keep a diary or journal. By second grade, most children should be confident enough in their writing abilities to communicate simple thoughts in writing. As they learn that they can relate their experiences and feelings in writing, they'll become eager to learn the words they want to use in their writing. Don't look at the journal without your child's permission. *If you're allowed to look but you can't read what she's written, ask her what she wrote. Don't correct* *spelling unless she asks you if she spelled specific words correctly.*

Word Sounds

Word sounds continue to be an important part of the second grade curriculum in most schools, and they also appear on most standardized tests. Skills include knowing how to identify vowel sounds and both initial and final consonant sounds.

Identifying Initial Consonant Sounds

A first grader's early confusion with initial consonant sounds will, by middle to late second grade, give way to sophisticated abilities to recognize single and multiple consonant sounds at the beginning of words.

Final Consonant Sounds

When they were in first grade, most children were confused by many word ending sounds, partly due to confusion over the word *ending*. Due to the cognitive development children experience at around age 7, most second graders suddenly develop very sophisticated abilities to identify ending word sounds. Most, for example, are able to achieve a high degree of accuracy in identifying single-consonant endings and consonant blends (like so<u>ng</u>).

Matching Vowel Sounds

Early readers see vowels as little more than place-holders. English is a language with complicated and sometimes unpredictable rules for vowel sounds that can stump many early readers. But the parts of the brain that govern sophisticated vowel sounds undergo tremendous development from ages 6 through 8.

By late second grade, most children know what vowels are and are able to identify basic vowel sounds such as the "o" sound in "dog." They are also able to identify different sounds made by the same vowels (such as the "o" sounds in "hog" and "both") and sounds made by vowel combinations, such as in "soap," "meat," and "tear."

What Tests May Ask

Standardized tests include questions on both vowel and consonant sounds. Questions may include attempts to distract the child with similar sounds. Although many first graders succumb to such deviousness, by late second grade most students should be adept enough at identifying ending sounds that they can confidently pick the correct answer from similar-sounding choices. For example, most second graders are able to discern that both "ch" and "tch" can make the same sound.

Practice Skill: Word Sounds

Directions: Which pair of words <u>begins</u> with the same sound?

1
  Ⓐ bat   place
  Ⓑ city   catch
  Ⓒ get   gypsy
  Ⓓ car   keep

2
  Ⓐ church   cool
  Ⓑ thin   tree
  Ⓒ care   kettle
  Ⓓ jug   go

3 Choose the word that has the same <u>beginning</u> sound as in <u>bread</u>.
  Ⓐ place
  Ⓑ bridge
  Ⓒ acre
  Ⓓ print

4 Choose the word with the same beginning sound as <u>cool</u>.

- Ⓐ kitchen
- Ⓑ school
- Ⓒ pine
- Ⓓ go

5 Which of these words has the same <u>ending</u> sound as in <u>head</u>?

- Ⓐ deal
- Ⓑ road
- Ⓒ heat
- Ⓓ meal

6 Which of these words has the same <u>ending</u> sound as in <u>poach</u>?

- Ⓐ bass
- Ⓑ fish
- Ⓒ notch
- Ⓓ beat

7 Which word has the same <u>vowel</u> sound as in <u>toad</u>?

- Ⓐ tooth
- Ⓑ rode
- Ⓒ top
- Ⓓ head

(See page 113 for answer key.)

Word Recognition

In second grade, your child will begin to recognize many new words when she hears them, and there will be an explosion in the number of words she recognizes by sight. The brain structures required to understand spoken and written words develop at a rapid pace during this period. Once your child begins to read independently, she experiences more new words, including words she's heard before but never read.

By late second grade, your child's confidence in her ability to read will allow her to guess the meaning of an unfamiliar word from its context. For example, if she reads the sentence: "The crew members held onto their seats when the captain ordered the spaceship into *reverse*," she can figure out from the rest of the sentence that something changed in the way the spaceship was traveling. She can then sound out the word to find further clues to the meaning of the word "reverse."

Many schools encourage early familiarization with dictionaries, which also encourages word recognition skills. Well-read second graders are especially strong at recognizing new words. The typical words that second graders learn are simple one- and two-syllable words that either follow standard phonetic rules or are very common.

Practice Skill: Word Recognition

Directions: Choose the word that means the same as the definitions in the following examples:

8 A stick that starts a fire when we rub it against something rough.

- Ⓐ watch
- Ⓑ stick
- Ⓒ fire
- Ⓓ match

9 Cook bread.

- Ⓐ sew
- Ⓑ catch
- Ⓒ make
- Ⓓ bake

10 Move a car.

Ⓐ sleep

Ⓑ drive

Ⓒ iron

Ⓓ jump

(See page 113 for answer key.)

Word Study: Compound Words

By second grade, most children come to realize that we readily alter words for different uses and combine two or more words to make new words, sometimes with meanings that have nothing to do with the original words. These combined words are called compound words.

For example, hotdogs aren't made from dogs, and they aren't necessarily hot. Hushpuppies—those crunchy fried bits of dough found throughout the South—aren't made from puppies, although they were originally developed to make the dogs "hush" when they bothered the cook who was preparing meals.

Second graders are learning that many words in English have been modified and combined to use in a new way. For example, we may take a noun and use it as a verb, such as when we use the noun "roller blade" as a verb: "Let's go rollerblading!" We do the same thing when we take a product name and use it as a verb in a way that drives manufacturers to distraction: "Go Xerox this contract" when we mean "Copy this on the copy machine"; or "Get a Kleenex for that runny nose" when we mean "Get a tissue."

Second graders also learn about verb endings to indicate tense, such as changing a verb to the past tense by adding "ed," as in, "Today I watch. Yesterday I watched."

Practice Skill: Word Study

Directions: Choose the correct answers for the following questions.

11 Choose the word that is made up of two words.

Ⓐ soccer

Ⓑ scarecrow

Ⓒ falcon

Ⓓ loosen

12 Choose the word that is made up of two words.

Ⓐ birdbath

Ⓑ running

Ⓒ harmony

Ⓓ robin

Directions: Choose the correct word to go in the blank in these sentences.

13 Today I mix paint. Yesterday I also ___ some.

Ⓐ mixer

Ⓑ mixture

Ⓒ mixed

Ⓓ mix

14 I like to ride horseback. Yesterday I _____ on a pony.

Ⓐ riding

Ⓑ rode

Ⓒ rided

Ⓓ ridded

(See page 113 for answer key.)

Contractions

While children learn to speak in contractions, typically they only begin to receive formal instruction in contractions during first grade. Even then, the instruction emphasizes simple, basic combinations such as "can + not = can't."

In contrast to the tentative grasp first graders have of such contractions, most second graders can use basic contractions fluently and can identify the words that were combined to form the contractions.

What Tests May Ask

Standardized tests in second grade include questions on contractions. Contractions are presented in two ways: by asking children to choose the original words making up a contraction, and by presenting two words and asking children to choose the correct contraction.

Practice Skill: Contractions

Directions: Choose the words that were combined to make the following contractions.

15 isn't
   Ⓐ is now
   Ⓑ is not
   Ⓒ is it
   Ⓓ did it

16 didn't
   Ⓐ did it
   Ⓑ did not
   Ⓒ will not
   Ⓓ do not

17 What contraction means the same as "does not"?
   Ⓐ doesn't
   Ⓑ didn't
   Ⓒ doe'snt
   Ⓓ do'esnt

18 What contraction means the same as "cannot?"
   Ⓐ ca'nt
   Ⓑ couldn't
   Ⓒ can't
   Ⓓ cann't

(See page 113 for answer key.)

Root Words and Suffixes

Root words are the original forms of words that we made into other words by adding a prefix or suffix. For example, the root word in "loudest" is "loud." By age 7, most children have become sufficiently sophisticated that they can identify the root words of many words they speak; this skill transfers very readily to words they read and write.

Most second graders are able to identify common root words, such as *count* in *counting* and *long* in *longest*. In fact, they recognize the term *root word* and understand its meaning because their teachers use the term.

Suffixes are word endings, such as the "ese" in "Chinese" and the "or" in "executor." Although many early second graders are confused by this concept, by late second grade most students are able to identify common suffixes. In many cases they are also able to state the meaning of the suffix; for example, "or" means "one who," as in "An exterminator is one who exterminates."

What Tests May Ask

Standardized tests include questions on both root words and suffixes. In some cases, students will be asked to identify the root word or suffix from a group of given words. Some will be tricky, such as understanding that "house" is the root word for "housing" even though the "e" has been dropped.

Practice Skill: Root Words and Suffixes

Directions: What is the root word in the following underlined words?

19 <u>sweetest</u>

    Ⓐ sweetening

    Ⓑ sweeter

    Ⓒ sweet

    Ⓓ sweeten

20 <u>housing</u>

    Ⓐ housed

    Ⓑ house

    Ⓒ home

    Ⓓ hous

21 <u>happiest</u>

    Ⓐ happi

    Ⓑ happier

    Ⓒ happy

    Ⓓ hoppy

Directions: Identify the <u>suffix</u> in each of the following underlined words.

22 <u>allowing</u>

    Ⓐ al

    Ⓑ allow

    Ⓒ ing

    Ⓓ low

23 <u>Japanese</u>

    Ⓐ Ja

    Ⓑ anese

    Ⓒ pan

    Ⓓ ese

24 What suffix do we add to the word <u>teach</u> to mean "one who teaches"?

    Ⓐ er

    Ⓑ ated

    Ⓒ ed

    Ⓓ taught

(See page 113 for answer key.)

CHAPTER 3

Vocabulary

The increase in your child's vocabulary that began in kindergarten and first grade will continue at full speed in second grade. The neural structures governing the ability to understand the vocabulary others use and the ability to express thoughts are still going through tremendous development, with corresponding increases in skills.

What Your Second Grader Should Be Learning

Most second graders are fluent English speakers, able to discuss a wide variety of subjects and understand what others say about many topics. Your child is beginning to understand abstract concepts when others discuss them, and he'll be struggling to use abstract and complex concepts himself.

Most second graders also have a well-developed picture vocabulary (the ability to match words and pictures). By second grade, your child will begin to understand more sophisticated pictures of abstract concepts; when he sees a picture of a person sitting with head in hands, he can say the picture shows sorrow. When he hears the term *conflict,* he can correctly choose from among a series of pictures one of two people arguing.

While most second graders do not understand the terms "synonym" and "antonym," they are able to understand the concept that two words can have either an opposite or a nearly identical meaning.

What You and Your Child Can Do

The single most effective way to strengthen a child's vocabulary skills is to read to him. Set aside a regular time each day to read books on a wide range of subjects; ask your child to choose. If Sam has an interest in astronomy, read about the moon and the planets. If Jeff came back from the beach with an interest in sea shells, read about the sea.

At the same time, encourage your child to start reading independently. Take regular trips with him to the bookstore and the library, and encourage him to read on a wide variety of subjects. Take him to places where he can expand his interests, where he can not only find more reading materials but also meet others who share his interests. If he's interested in comic books, take him to a comic book convention. Join the local zoo society if animals interest him. Subscribe to magazines dealing with his hobbies. There is a growing market of magazines in many areas of interest at a reading level appropriate for second graders. As he reads about the things that interest him, your child's vocabulary will grow.

Talk. Talk to your child. He will become more comfortable with all aspects of language in direct proportion to his exposure to it. Extensive research has shown that children with a strong vocabulary have parents with the same skills. Parents with solid vocabulary skills tend to use a technique that linguists refer to as "scaffolding" with their children.

For example, Adam's mother tells him: "I hope the snow waits until after you're out of school today. If they have to dismiss school early, it'll be *pandemonium. Kids will be running around all over the place, and everything will be confused.*" Without advertising the fact, Adam's mother uses a big word and defines it within the context of the sentence.

It's also quite appropriate for you to define words outright when you talk to your child. For example, if Henry's mother is showing him how to weave fish nets, she may say, "Now we put the shuttle through here and make a *sheet bend*. A sheet bend is a knot like this" (demonstrating the knot). Or Jamie's father might say something like, "Your great-grandfather was a *haberdasher.* That's someone who makes hats."

Learn New Words. Let your second grader see you take an interest in learning new words. If you're reading the newspaper and come across a word you don't know, let your child see you look it up. Go to the dictionary; if it's not there, get on the Internet and find it. Encourage your child to do the same thing. If he comes across a word, help him look it up in an age-appropriate dictionary. Make flash cards with words that your children struggle with, and drill them. You can also obtain words from the state word list for second grade.

Picture Vocabulary

Second graders should be old hands at identifying pictures. Remember your toddler's delight at saying, "Horsie!" when you opened a storybook to a picture of a horse. Until about second grade, children's picture identification skills have mostly been restricted to naming objects in pictures.

Most children should enter second grade able to identify very simple abstract words from pictures, such as choosing the picture of the person with a broad smile as the happy one among four other pictures. By second grade, children begin

to understand more sophisticated abstract concepts.

What Tests May Ask

In standardized tests for second grade, students will be asked to interpret pictures by choosing the correct word that the picture represents. Questions will present a picture and ask for the appropriate description from a group of possibilities; or present a word and ask children to choose the correct picture that represents that word.

Practice Skill: Picture Vocabulary

Directions: Choose the correct answer in the following questions.

1 How does the girl in this picture feel?

    Ⓐ sorry

    Ⓑ proud

    Ⓒ regret

    Ⓓ brave

2 Which of the following pictures shows *caring*?

Ⓐ

Ⓑ

Ⓒ

Ⓓ

(See page 113 for answer key.)

Vocabulary Development

When your child was younger, he sometimes had trouble choosing the right word for what he wanted to say. For example, Jim might announce, "Jim got hot," when he means that he has a fever. As your child enters second grade, he will begin to develop the ability to describe thoughts and feelings much more precisely.

What Tests May Ask

Standardized tests for second graders assess vocabulary development in several ways. Most often, the tests present sentences with a word missing, and ask children to fill in the blank with a correct word from a group of choices.

Practice Skills: Vocabulary Development

Directions: Choose the correct word to go in the blank in these sentences.

3 The puppy dug a hole to _____ the bone.
- Ⓐ dig
- Ⓑ bone
- Ⓒ hole
- Ⓓ bury

4 There was no computer left for T. J. to use to play the game. Kara told him, "Come over here and we can _____."
- Ⓐ look
- Ⓑ cooperate
- Ⓒ study
- Ⓓ share

(See page 113 for answer key.)

Synonyms and Antonyms

Most second graders don't understand the term *synonym*, but almost all understand the concept of two words that mean the same thing. Most can quite accurately make simple comparisons, such as *big* and *large*. Because your child is making progress in understanding abstract and complex terms, he will be able to identify some synonyms referring to basic abstract words.

For example, your child will probably be able to tell you that "rich" and "wealthy" mean the same thing. In contrast to your first grader, who was fooled into thinking that words like "purse" and "pocketbook" are different, your second grader will be much more flexible and will understand that these two words refer to the same object. On the other hand, he may be confused by one-way relationships, such as noting that all eagles are birds, but not all birds are eagles.

Most children are intrigued by words that mean the opposite in first grade. At that age, however, their understanding of similarities and differences among words is largely limited to concrete comparisons relying on tangible properties, such as "up" versus "down."

By middle to late second grade, students begin to understand more complex and abstract comparisons. For example, second graders learn to recognize that "weak" means the opposite of "strong" and "expensive" means the opposite of "cheap." In most schools, they won't learn the term *antonym* until third or fourth grade, but most second graders will be able to identify opposites with a high degree of accuracy.

What Tests May Ask

Standardized tests for second graders assess a child's understanding of opposites and similarities by asking youngsters to choose a synonym or antonym for an underlined word in a sentence from among a group of possibilities.

Practice Skill: Synonyms and Antonyms

Directions: Look at the underlined word in each sentence. Which word is a <u>synonym</u> (a word that means the same thing) for the underlined word?

5 Paula <u>grinned</u> when she heard the good news.
   Ⓐ smiled
   Ⓑ laughed
   Ⓒ gained
   Ⓓ grew

6 When it got dark, we heard the <u>cry</u> of a wolf.
   Ⓐ laugh
   Ⓑ howl
   Ⓒ yell
   Ⓓ bark

Directions: Look at the sentences and pick the word that means the <u>opposite</u> of the word that is underlined.

7 Josh's experiment was a <u>success</u>.
   Ⓐ achievement
   Ⓑ happy
   Ⓒ experiment
   Ⓓ failure

8 Amy <u>forgot</u> Elena's telephone number.

   Ⓐ missed

   Ⓑ learned

   Ⓒ telephone

   Ⓓ remembered

9 Bill was <u>sad</u> that his team lost the game.

   Ⓐ angry

   Ⓑ happy

   Ⓒ jealous

   Ⓓ surprised

(See page 113 for answer key.)

Words in Context

Remember when your child began reading by calling words in a mechanical, choppy fashion? He would frequently read at the same monotonous rate, without any change in the pace or tone of the dialogue. He would keep reading even if he used a wrong word that made no sense given the other elements of the sentence.

By second grade, because your child no longer struggles with reading every word, he is becoming more aware of cadence and tone. He will stop when he reads a word that doesn't make sense within the sentence. At this stage, he is developing a skill called "closure": the ability to understand the total meaning of the combined elements of sentences. As your child gets older, he'll become better at filling in missing elements and detecting words that don't belong in the sentence.

What Tests May Ask

Standardized tests at this age assess your child's ability to understand words in context by presenting sentences and asking students to choose the best word to complete the sentence.

Practice Skill: Words in Context

Directions: Read each sentence and choose the word that should go in the blank.

10 It was time to eat supper, so Maria _____ her bicycle home.

   Ⓐ bicycle

   Ⓑ home

   Ⓒ rode

   Ⓓ played

11 Jimmy looked all over the place. He could not ___ the green crayon.

   Ⓐ buy

   Ⓑ crayon

   Ⓒ color

   Ⓓ find

12 As the rain clouds gathered, Sharon _____ the boat to the dock.

   Ⓐ sailed

   Ⓑ swam

   Ⓒ walked

   Ⓓ ate

(See page 113 for answer key.)

Multi-Meaning Words

Many words have more than one meaning. For example, "rest" can mean the same as "remainder" or "what you do when you're tired." Younger children can be quite inflexible with such words and insist that "can" means something we open to get soup and does not mean the same as "is able."

By second grade, children have encountered such a wide variety of uses of different words and are becoming so flexible that they are able to allow for the possibility that a word can have multiple meanings. But because they are still developing this skill, it's not at all unusual for second graders to sometimes be moderately frustrated.

Practice Skill: Multi-Meaning Words

Directions: Here are two sets of sentences. Choose the correct word that should go in the blanks in both sentences.

13 James did not want all of the popcorn, so he let me have the _____. Mary sat down to _____ before she finished the hike.

   (A) popcorn   (B) sit

   (C) down   (D) rest

14 Jeffrey was not able to open the _____ of soup. We should find out if Lisa _____ open it.

   (A) bowl   (B) can

   (C) could   (D) will

(See page 113 for answer key.)

CHAPTER 4

Reading Comprehension

Second grade is the time when most elementary schools (and standardized tests) begin to put a heavy emphasis on reading comprehension.

What Your Second Grader Should Be Learning

While first graders struggle word by word simply to complete the mechanical act of identifying words, most second graders are more secure in this ability and can begin to put together the total meaning of a story from the elements of sentences and paragraphs. During this year, most students begin to appreciate humor and irony (although they probably won't understand the latter term). They begin to critically evaluate what they read.

Second graders are becoming discerning readers, and are beginning to understand the difference between fantasy and reality. They are also becoming better able to infer reality from pictures and photos, as their picture comprehension increases. They are becoming better able to pick out the implied feelings and motivations of characters they read about, and can select a title for a paragraph or brief story that indicates the ability to pick out the key points in what they've read.

What You and Your Child Can Do

If you've been reading to your child since she was young, you've already built a strong foundation for all areas of reading. By now she's become accustomed to following along and understanding the events as you read. As she is reading on her own more and more, she is learning to expect that the details she reads will form a well-developed story line.

Continue reading to her and let her read to you. Follow the advice in Chapters 2 and 3: Ask her about what she reads.

Magazines. Subscribe to age-appropriate magazines such as *Ranger Rick, Stone Soup,* or *Junior Scholastic.* Your child will find new areas of interest, often things she never knew would interest her.

Newspapers. Encourage your child to read a variety of books, magazines, and newspapers on a variety of subjects. Point out short articles in the newspaper or your magazines that you think would interest her. If she has trouble reading the articles, help her. Enjoy reading together.

Sunday newspapers often have children's sections that cover some of the events in the news or profile notable people. Reading these, children learn that they can obtain interesting and useful information from newspapers. Particularly if they see you reading newspapers, magazines, nonfiction, and fiction for pleasure, they'll want to begin to do the same.

Let your child see you read for information related to your home or your job. If you're planning to buy a computer, tell her why you went to the bookstore and bought a buyer's guide to computers. Involve her in looking through the specifications and descriptions of each brand and model.

If there are trade magazines that cater to your profession, let your child see you reading them, and explain to her why you read them. Seeing you read to obtain information reinforces the idea that reading is important.

Library Visits. As your child gets older, she'll want to choose her own books. Schedule regular trips to the library, but once you're there, go off and look for your own books and let her browse on her own. Most libraries give cards to children who are old enough to sign their names.

Having a library card can be a first important step in learning responsibility. Teach your child early to ask the librarians for help, and how to use the computer terminals or card catalog to locate books.

You can afford to give some gentle guidance in the books your child chooses, but let her have the final choice. Forbid books only if you think the subject matter is inappropriate.

Get Advice. Encourage your second grader to read books that require her to understand characters, appreciate suspense, and anticipate action. Get recommendations from her teacher, the school librarian, or the children's librarian at your local library. Look for books in a series that emphasize character and plot development.

Picture Comprehension

Second graders still look for pictures in their books. Pictures can provide clues to the story and can help clarify parts of what students read. Kindergartners and many first graders simply look for a basic listing of elements in pictures, with some minor interpretation of action, such as, "There are two girls and two boys and a birthday cake. It is somebody's birthday."

Second graders will begin to be able to read more sophisticated details into pictures and to interpret what facial expressions, subtle action,

and other elements imply. For example, if a photo shows a politician giving a speech and the aide standing behind is rolling her eyes, most second graders are able to detect that she doesn't believe what the politician is saying.

Second graders also begin to develop the ability to anticipate what will happen next from the depicted elements.

Practice Skill: Picture Comprehension

Directions: Look at the following picture and answer the question about the picture.

1 How did the pirate feel when he opened the treasure box?
   Ⓐ scared and surprised
   Ⓑ happy
   Ⓒ sad and lonely
   Ⓓ rich

Ⓐ

Ⓑ

Ⓒ

Ⓓ

2 Which picture shows what will happen next?

(See page 113 for answer key.)

Critical Reading

Very young readers accept what they read literally: If it's written down, it must be true. In the 1950s, many first graders believed in Dick, Jane, Sally, their dog Spot, and their cat Puff. By second grade, many children have become more realistic. They recognize that pirates no longer roam the seas and that science fiction is just that—fiction. By this age, your child is beginning to discern reality from fantasy in what she sees on television, in the stories you read to her, and in what she herself reads.

By second grade, your child can probably draw conclusions from what she reads. If the author presents a number of facts to support the notion that walking is good exercise, many second graders will draw the conclusion that walking can be a beneficial form of exercise.

Your second grader will also begin to understand characters. Although she tends to see characters in black-and-white terms, she will gradually begin to understand that bad characters aren't all bad and that good characters have flaws. Just as she begins to see people around her in an increasingly complex way, she will gradually be able to extend those skills to her reading.

For example, she may read about Pretty Boy Floyd and learn that he was a notorious bank robber who fed the poor and paid off farm mortgages to prevent foreclosure. She will be able to see that rather than being a comic-book bad guy, Floyd had some good points.

By second grade, most children are beginning to understand the difference between fact and opinion. Most second graders still struggle with subtle distinctions between the two, but they should be able to discriminate fact from opinion in blatant examples.

Practice Skill: Critical Reading

Directions: Choose the correct answers for the following questions.

3 Which of these sentences is true?
- (A) Humans have walked on the moon.
- (B) Humans have walked on the sun.
- (C) Humans live on Mars.
- (D) Pirates live on big ships.

Directions: Read this sentence and then answer the question.

4 The teacher sent Jeffrey to the office for shooting Ellen with a rubber band. As Jeffrey left, he said, "But I didn't do it." Tom grinned as he saw Jeffrey leave the class and thought to himself, "I got away with it." Who shot Ellen with a rubber band?
- (A) Tom
- (B) Jeffrey
- (C) Ellen
- (D) the teacher

5 Terrell always picked on the other children. No one wanted to play with him. What they did not know was that Terrell's brother and his friends always picked on Terrell at home. Why do you think Terrell picked on other boys and girls?
- (A) Others at home always picked on him.
- (B) He was bad.
- (C) He was a boy.
- (D) He did not speak English.

6 The Nasty Company is run by bad men. They make cleaning products. They don't have any women bosses. They had to pay a million dollars last year because they were caught polluting the Smith River. Now choose which of these sentences tells the writer's <u>opinion</u>.

Ⓐ The Nasty Company is run by bad men.

Ⓑ They make cleaning products.

Ⓒ They do not have any women bosses.

Ⓓ They had to pay a million dollars last year because they were caught polluting the Smith River.

(See page 113 for answer key.)

Story Comprehension

Along with improvement in the ability to recognize words, in second grade comes an improvement in the ability to understand stories. No longer do children have to struggle through books, stumbling over every other word they read. No longer do they plod monotonously through the sentences in a robotic fashion.

One of the earliest abilities second graders recognize is the ability to discriminate details. They are able to glean a character's height, build, likes, dislikes, and actions if the writer discusses them and they have a bearing on the story. They are able to understand details about the setting and the time in which the story takes place.

They also develop an ability to make inferences. If a character says, "I will let you keep the puppy—for now," second graders understand that the character is implying that she may make the other character get rid of the puppy later. They begin to understand foreshadowing. If one character says, "I just know that we can trust Mr. Jones to do the right thing," and the main character frowns upon hearing this, second graders gather that we may not be able to trust Mr. Jones.

Second graders begin to understand environmental changes that authors introduce to foreshadow. For example, if the skies grow dark and the birds stop singing when Aunt Jean comes for a visit, they are able to tell that Aunt Jean's visit might not be a good thing.

One of the more important abilities children begin developing in second grade is the ability to understand what unfamiliar words mean. For example, if the story has just given many examples of Angela's negative attitude—constant criticism, violence, and sharp speech—second graders will more readily figure out the meaning of "sarcastic" in the sentence, "Rob couldn't understand why Angela was being so sarcastic."

Now when your child encounters unfamiliar words, she will be better able to fill in the gaps in her understanding and will be better able to figure out the correct meaning of words she looks up in a dictionary. For example, if you said you needed to put a leaf in the table when company comes for dinner, your second grader could look up "leaf" in the dictionary and understand its meaning in this context.

Second graders also begin to develop the ability to figure out an author's purpose. For example, if a story begins with a man being sent to prison but then emphasizes all his good deeds and all the bad things his accusers do, many second graders are able to figure out that the author is trying to show that the man is good and his accusers are bad.

Many second graders enjoy reading stories like Aesop's Fables. While younger children are unable to appreciate the deeper meanings embedded in fables, second graders can apply the meaning of these stories to their lives. For example, if a child reads *The Beauty and the Beast*, she will be able to explain the lesson that we shouldn't judge others by their outward appearances.

Children at this age also begin to more fully appreciate the sequence of ideas and the buildup of suspense. They more readily appreciate the sequence of events in nonfiction, such as when they read stories about how the American colonies defeated the British in the American Revolution or how the North defeated the South in the Civil War. In later grades, their ability to appreciate character and plot development will grow.

During second grade, your child will begin to develop the ability to come up with alternate titles for stories she reads or watches on TV. For example, one second grader referred to the movie *Close Encounters of the Third Kind* as *We Meet Martians*. The ability to provide titles for stories requires relatively sophisticated reading comprehension skills that generally only begin at about second grade.

The ability to provide a title for a reading is important because it's closely related to the ability to understand a story's main idea. Younger readers understand a sentence or at most a paragraph at a time; but second graders can put together the sentences and paragraphs to understand the passage's main idea.

Your second grader is becoming a more sophisticated reader in yet another sense: She understands and infers subtle emotional clues. The ability to understand a character's feelings involves not only understanding the words presented but also drawing inferences from sometimes subtle wording and implied action. Most early second graders struggle with identifying feelings other than those that are blatantly presented. For example, unless the author specifically says, "Jennifer was sad," many early second graders won't understand the feelings reflected in passages like this:

As Jennifer's mother welcomed Uncle Bob, Jennifer sighed and turned away.

By middle to late second grade, most students begin to develop stronger abilities to draw inferences regarding characters' feelings from more subtle information.

Practice Skill: Story Comprehension

Directions: Read the following brief story and then answer the questions.

Story: Jeffrey saw a man he had never met. "Jeffrey," his mother said, "this is your Uncle Robert." Jeffrey started to say hello, but his dog Baxter ran toward Uncle Robert, growling. Jeffrey's mother said, "What's wrong with Baxter? He never growls at people."

7 What do you think the author is trying to tell you?

Ⓐ Baxter is a bad dog.

Ⓑ Jeffrey is a bad boy.

Ⓒ Uncle Robert does not like Jeffrey.

Ⓓ Uncle Robert might be a bad man.

Directions: Read the stories below and answer the questions that follow.

Story: Wanda and Lisa could never kick the soccer ball straight, so they never scored any points in the games they played. Wanda went home from school every day and watched television, but Lisa started practicing every day. Her brother made her a net in their backyard, and every day after school she practiced kicking the soccer ball into the net from different places in the yard. Her brother blocked her shots so that she learned how to kick around him. Pretty soon, Lisa started scoring points in every soccer game she played. Wanda never got any better.

8 What is the lesson in this story?

Ⓐ If you want something a lot, you'll get it.

Ⓑ If you don't get something you want, it is not fair.

Ⓒ Practice makes perfect.

Ⓓ Wanda was lazy.

Story: Sharon and Leslie were twin sisters. They lived in a house by the river. One day, Sharon saw her father fall into the river. He called for help. Sharon ran and told Leslie, "Daddy fell in the river. Come help!" Sharon tied one end of a rope around a tree. Leslie tied the other end around a stick and threw it to their father. He grabbed the rope and was able to pull himself back to the bank and get out of the river.

9 What is a good title for this story?

Ⓐ Sharon and Leslie Rescue Their Father

Ⓑ Sharon and Leslie Lived by a River

Ⓒ Sharon and Leslie's Father Went Fishing

Ⓓ Sharon and Leslie Were Twins

Story: My sister bought a Dream Catcher at the Ojibwa Indian Reservation. It's a round hoop covered in leather string with a net inside the hoop that has a hole in the middle. The lady who made it told my sister that she would attach a string of beads and a feather so they fell across the hole. She said that the Ojibwa believe that if you hang the Dream Catcher over your bed, it catches dreams in the net. The good dreams find the beads and the feather and slide down so that you can dream them. The bad dreams get caught in the net and die.

10 Why do the Ojibwa make Dream Catchers?

Ⓐ They use them to fight their enemies in war.

Ⓑ They believe that they will bring good dreams.

Ⓒ They have to do something with all their beads and feathers.

Ⓓ They try to see who can make the biggest one.

Story: Larry's mother said, "Come over here, Larry, and let me measure you." Larry came over and stood against the door frame and his mother measured his height. Then she asked Larry to measure her height. They were the same. "Larry," she said, "you are as tall as I am." Larry said, "No big deal," and turned and walked away. But, as he walked away, he was grinning.

11 How do you think Larry felt?

- Ⓐ angry
- Ⓑ proud
- Ⓒ tall
- Ⓓ short

(See page 113 for answer key.)

CHAPTER 5

Listening

Children between the ages of about 6 and 8 experience tremendous development in the brain structures required for processing information they hear. (They don't always pay attention, but they can certainly understand.) This means your child is much better able to discriminate even subtle nuances in speech characteristics.

What Your Second Grader Should Be Learning

By second grade, your child's brain development helps him better interpret what he hears. As a result, he can better understand dialogue, listen to and be influenced by advertisements, and understand that song lyrics tell stories. His listening skills are becoming much more highly developed. Now second graders can follow story lines, process and interpret information, and pick out illogical elements in a logical flow of ideas.

What You and Your Child Can Do

If you've been following the suggestions for building reading skills by reading to your child, you have been automatically boosting his listening skills too. When your child becomes interested in the stories you read, he becomes more motivated to extract as much information as possible from the books.

He is also learning to critically evaluate what he hears, which will prepare him for future appreciation of plays, poetry, and songs.

Stories on Tape. You can find audio tapes to play in the car. Even a cursory examination of the library will reveal many popular books and classics on tape. Let Harrison Ford read *Treasure Island* to the family as you drive down the interstate. But don't simply rely on the professionals. Tape yourself reading your child's favorite books for those times when you aren't around and he wants to hear the stories *just one more time*. Listen to old radio shows on tape or CDs; you can find them at the library or bookstore.

Communicate. Talk to your children. Make time every day to discuss what's going on in his life. Share your feelings and the details of what's going well and what's going badly. Some parents only average about seven minutes a day talking with their children. That's just not enough.

Share Hobbies. Share your hobbies and interests with your child. Take him with you to stamp collector conventions and talk with him about why a particular stamp is rare. Let him help you catalog your pennies by matching them with labeled knock-outs in archive books. Let him sit with you when you peruse catalogs, and tell him why you want one product, why you would never use another product, and what you plan to do with the items you are ordering.

Act Up! Enjoy poetry and plays with your children. Ask your child to retell the stories to check whether he understands what he has heard, and reread passages that he misunderstands or can't remember.

Sports on Air. When you watch sports on TV with your child, turn down the sound and listen to the coverage on the radio. Remember: Radio commentators must use more vivid and colorful descriptions than TV commentators because their audience can't see the action.

Listening Skills

An important listening skill emerges when children can match what they hear and what they see: the ability to look at a group of pictures and pick out the ones that go with descriptions they hear. For example, Julia's mother hands her a catalog turned to a page with nine objects pictured on it and asks, "Julia, do you think Daddy would like this golf bag for his birthday?" If the page has eight other golf-related products and only one golf bag, Julia must be able to discriminate that only the bag, not the spike cleaner, the ball washer, or the golf towel matches the phrase *golf bag*.

An outgrowth of the ability to identify pictures from their elements at this age is the ability to classify them. Classifying requires subtle interpretation skills that were largely missing at younger ages. Although younger children can begin to classify pictures according to criteria they hear based on concrete qualities such as quantity, size, and color, children between the ages of 7 and 8 begin to strengthen their abilities to classify according to more subtle characteristics.

What Tests May Ask

Standardized tests of listening skills require children to answer questions based on sentences, phrases, or stories they have read and to identify pictures from their elements.

Practice Skill: Listening Skills

Directions: (Read this to your child): "Tom went out into the rain without his rain coat."

1 Which one is Tom?

 Ⓐ

 Ⓑ

 Ⓒ

 Ⓓ

Directions: Read the questions and the possible answers to your child.

2 What is happening in this picture?

Ⓐ Lana fell on her bicycle and skinned her knee.

Ⓑ Terrell got a new bicycle for his birthday.

Ⓒ Linda won the bicycle race.

Ⓓ Keisha ran faster than the others.

3 Which picture shows the person who is the happiest?

Ⓐ

Ⓑ

Ⓒ

Ⓓ

4 What happened to Samantha?

- Ⓐ She had bad luck.
- Ⓑ She became angry at her brother Teddy.
- Ⓒ She had good luck.
- Ⓓ She made a new friend.

(See page 113 for answer key.)

Language Skills

Most second graders begin to develop much stronger listening comprehension skills (the ability to process and interpret what they hear). In contrast to younger children, who watch television passively enjoying action, children at this age show much stronger abilities to understand, follow, and retell story lines they hear.

Another important listening skill that develops during this period is the ability to discriminate the logical flow of ideas and to be able to identify elements that don't belong.

What Tests May Ask

The type of question standardized tests use to assess listening comprehension ability asks students to listen to a passage and then answer questions about it. The tests may also ask children to remember specific details of a passage and to integrate them with what they have previously learned.

Practice Skill: Language Skills

Directions: Read this to your child:

Listen to this commercial and then I will ask you questions about what you hear.

COMMERCIAL

Hey, boys and girls, don't miss the chance to win a free mountain bike! All you have to do is send in a completed entry form from the back of a Snow Flakes Cereal box. Snow Flakes—the first cereal to be made completely of sugar! Just get Mom or Dad to cut out the entry form from the back of any specially marked box of Snow Flakes with a picture of Kenny the Cavity on it, get them to help you fill out the form, and send it along with the tops from five specially marked boxes of Snow Flakes to the address shown on the form. Two hundred lucky boys and girls will win Crasho Mountain Bikes when the drawing is held during the halftime program at the Super Bowl. Limit one entry per child.

Directions: Read the questions and answers below to your child.

5 What cereal has the entry forms for the contest?
- Ⓐ Boingos
- Ⓑ Shrunken Heads
- Ⓒ Monster Mania
- Ⓓ Snow Flakes

6 What did the announcer say that is wrong or is silly?

Ⓐ Snow Flakes has all the daily vitamins and minerals a growing boy or girl needs.

Ⓑ The drawing will be held during the halftime at the Super Bowl.

Ⓒ Snow Flakes is made totally of sugar.

Ⓓ Have Mom or Dad help you cut out and complete the entry form.

7 How many boys and girls will win bicycles?

Ⓐ One boy and one girl

Ⓑ Two hundred boys and girls

Ⓒ Two hundred boys

Ⓓ Two hundred girls

Directions: Read this direction, the following questions, and the answers to your child:

"Choose the word that is wrong in each of these sentences."

8 It was time for Scotty's dog Chipper to get his shots, so Scotty took Chipper to the dentist.

Ⓐ shots

Ⓑ Chipper

Ⓒ dentist

Ⓓ veterinarian

9 Kim's parents are veterinarians. They do not eat meat.

Ⓐ parents

Ⓑ veterinarians

Ⓒ meat

Ⓓ eat

(See page 113 for answer key.)

CHAPTER 6

Language Mechanics

Remember when your children were first learning to read? Early readers tend to read in a monotonous, robot-like fashion, never stopping for periods or paragraphs and not distinguishing which words are proper nouns.

By second grade, your child is becoming much more aware of the sounds of writing. The child who in first grade saw capitalization as arbitrary and punctuation marks as some sort of mystical scribbling will begin how to understand why we capitalize and punctuate.

What Your Second Grader Should Be Learning

The first skill your child will master is that of capitalizing proper nouns. By the end of second grade, she should begin to accurately discriminate which nouns require capitalization. At this age, she probably won't understand some of the more sophisticated capitalization rules, such as capitalizing the first letter of the first word of an independent clause following a colon. She will probably often be confused by the rules for which letters in titles are *not* capitalized, such as in *The Taming of the Shrew*. Last year, your child's teacher probably didn't stress capitalization beyond proper names or punctuation. The teacher may have talked about placing question marks at the end of interrogative sentences, but probably didn't require your child to demonstrate where to put them. First-grade teachers don't emphasize punctuation very much because they are more concerned with helping children

get used to putting their thoughts down on paper. At that age, for example, your child would have simply labeled a picture of a lion laughing as "Jolly Lion," usually in all capitals. By second grade, she should be comfortable enough with expressing simple thoughts that she can begin to learn more sophisticated elements of writing, including capitalization and punctuation.

What You and Your Child Can Do

The best way for children to learn language mechanics is to write. By second grade, most children can benefit from gentle correction of basic capitalization and punctuation errors. There are lots of ways you can get them to practice.

For example, ask your child to write a postcard to Aunt Irene telling her about a trip to the beach. Write the first draft with your child, and go over it with her to check for errors. Let her copy the words onto the postcard. When you return from the beach vacation, get her to write a story about her experiences and go over it gently again, pointing out blatant errors in capitalization and punctuation.

Don't worry at this age about sophisticated concepts such as colons, semicolons, dashes, quotation marks, and ellipses. For now, concentrate on:

- commas,
- periods,
- question marks, and
- exclamation points.

Start out with commas by emphasizing their use in separating elements of a series, but don't worry about teaching how to separate independent clauses until your child's teacher begins to emphasize this skill. Look over homework and class papers that come home, or call the teacher to see how the grammar instruction is progressing.

Keep a Diary. Encourage your child to keep a diary. There are attractive journals and diaries at stationery stores and bookstores, and they make nice gifts for children. Keeping a diary will allow your child to get used to writing down her feelings and experiences. This will prepare her for later capitalization and punctuation.

If your child sometimes uses your computer to compose stories, be sure to turn off automatic grammar flagging, which will only confuse younger children. It can become very frustrating to have the word processor stop after every few words to issue a flag. Encourage your child to write out her stories and reports by hand.

When you read your second grader's essay and find it contains many punctuation errors, ask her to read it out loud. Point out how the natural end points require periods, and that places where she pauses often require commas: It simply sounds right.

Capitalization

Capitalizing nouns is one of the first skills children learn in second grade. They learn that names for people, their school, and books, songs, movies, and TV programs begin with capital letters. At first they may find it hard to tell the difference between proper nouns and other nouns, and may mistakenly capitalize all nouns in sentences (such as, "My Dog Baxter ran down the Street"). By the end of second grade, your child should understand which nouns require capitalization.

At this age, your child will also become aware that sentences begin with capital letters. At first she may have trouble figuring out when sentences actually begin, and she may capitalize the first letter of the first word following a comma or a semicolon. Eventually, she'll improve on this skill as she begins to see the importance of capitalization.

What Tests May Ask

Because current standardized tests must assess capitalization skills in a way that can be scored by computer, they rely on a child's ability to recognize correct capitalization rather than produce it. Some computer-assisted testing procedures are now being developed that will allow children to enter their responses so that computers can assess expressive capitalization skills, but these aren't widely available now. As a result, standardized tests today ask fairly straightforward questions about punctuation and capitalization.

Practice Skill: Capitalization

Directions: Read these sentences. Then choose the word that needs to begin with capital letters.

1 We gave katie a kitten for her birthday.
   Ⓐ gave
   Ⓑ katie
   Ⓒ kitten
   Ⓓ birthday

2 did anyone find the book that I lost yesterday?
   Ⓐ anyone
   Ⓑ did
   Ⓒ book
   Ⓓ yesterday

3 We are going to the south of france.

Ⓐ going

Ⓑ south

Ⓒ france

Ⓓ we

---

4 Shall we go to peter's house on Friday?

Ⓐ peter's

Ⓑ house

Ⓒ shall

Ⓓ friday

(See page 113 for answer key.)

Punctuation

The first punctuation mark that children learn is the period as the ending mark of the sentence. Until about second grade, many children simply write stories and reports in one long sentence, never able to distinguish where one idea stops and another begins. They also tend to read passages as if they are all one long, run-on sentence, with no pauses for breath or dramatic effect.

Period

By second grade, your child should be much more comfortable making this distinction and should be able to easily identify where to put periods in simple, declarative sentences such as: "Johnny enjoyed baseball. Mary enjoyed soccer."

However, even by late second grade, many children are confused by compound sentences such as: "Johnny enjoyed baseball, but Mary enjoyed soccer." and use periods instead of commas.

Question Mark

The question mark is usually the second punctuation mark that children learn. Most children find the question mark easy because it's so simple to tell which sentences make statements and which ask questions.

Exclamation Mark

Look at a first grader's essays, and you'll see that many of her sentences end in exclamation marks. As children begin to experience the typical second grade emphases on writing, many early second graders continue to overuse exclamation points. To many younger children, *every* sentence makes a forceful statement, probably reflecting the exuberance they feel toward life in general.

To the world-weary adult, going to the lake for the weekend may only merit a period. But to a 7-year-old to whom the sky is so much bluer, perhaps "I went to the lake this weekend!" really deserves an exclamation mark. With greater experience in writing (certainly by middle to late second grade), most children are able to understand that not every statement is a forceful exclamation.

Now that schools are beginning to teach even first and second graders to use word processors, teachers have begun to notice that they must teach children that if every sentence is in bold type, the impact is lessened. In the same way, teachers have found over the years that they must convince children that if every sentence ends in an exclamation point, the impact is diluted.

Comma

Many second graders still find commas confusing. They understand that commas are used to separate members of a series ("John found two pennies, three flashlight batteries, and his sister's nail polish under the chair cushion."). Distinguishing when it's appropriate to use a comma or a semicolon to separate elements of a series will also typically confuse them. Be content in second grade to emphasize simple comma use.

Most second graders are particularly confused about when to use a comma and when to use a period between two independent clauses, and when to leave out the comma altogether. For example, when confronted with the sentences:

"Mary tried to call Kelly but forgot her telephone number."

or

"Mary tried to call Kelly, but she forgot her telephone number."

your child may be confused as to why the second sentence requires a comma but the first doesn't. Teachers have found that the terms "independent" and "dependent" clauses confuse children in the early grades. Experienced teachers emphasize that a comma goes between parts of sentences that are separated by a "connector" (conjunction) such as "and" or "but" if it can stand alone. For example, in the first of the two sentences above, the phrases "Mary tried to call Kelly" and "forgot her telephone number" can't both stand alone, so we don't put a comma between them when we join them with *but*. However, "Mary tried to call Kelly" and "she forgot her telephone number" can both stand alone, so when we join them with *but*, we put a comma between them.

What Tests May Ask

As with capitalization, the challenge in assessing punctuation skills with standardized tests is in presenting test items in a format that will allow children to answer them on scan sheets used to score them by computer. We must therefore rely on assessments that test a child's ability to recognize correct and incorrect punctuation when she sees it. Standardized tests frequently present three or four sentences and ask which one is punctuated correctly.

Practice Skills: Punctuation

Directions: Which of these sentences is punctuated correctly?

5 (A) Sally likes ice cream, but does not like cake.

(B) Donald can ride a bicycle but he needs training wheels.

(C) Jean washed, and waxed her mother's car.

(D) Jennifer washed her hands and dried them on the towel.

Directions: Choose where we need to add punctuation in this sentence.

6 Donald wanted to go to the zoo __
(A)
but __ his mother said __ that the
(B)   (C)
zoo __ was closed that day.
(D)

Directions: Choose the sentence with the correct punctuation.

7 (A) The girl ran to get the dog but couldn't unlock the gate.

(B) The girl, ran to get the dog, but couldn't unlock the gate.

(C) The girl ran to get the dog, but couldn't unlock the gate.

(D) The girl ran, to get the dog, but couldn't unlock the gate.

8 Ⓐ Swinging her pail, Jill ran down the hill.

Ⓑ Swinging her pail Jill ran down the hill.

Ⓒ Swinging, her pail Jill ran down, the hill.

Ⓓ Swinging her pail Jill ran, down the hill.

(See page 113 for answer key.)

Language Mechanics

Until now, we've emphasized the ability to decide when we should capitalize and punctuate in short examples. In the beginning, your child's second grade teacher will probably emphasize these skills in isolation, in the same way as in our examples.

But gradually (usually by late second grade to early third grade), children will begin to apply these same principles to longer passages that they read and write. They'll gradually develop a greater appreciation for the principles behind these skills and learn that by using them correctly, the writer helps the reader to understand what he's reading.

What Tests May Ask

Standardized tests assess capitalization and punctuation skills of longer passages in a format that allows them to use scanning sheets. The tests ask students to choose the correct single choice or to pick out the wrong choice from a group of correct responses.

Practice Skill: Language Mechanics

Directions: Read the following paragraph. Above each underlined phrase is a number that belongs to a question below the paragraph. Decide how each numbered phrase should be capitalized and punctuated.

Story: Lisa and her brother Ray
                    9   10
went to the <u>beach they</u> found <u>sea shells driftwood and even a shark's tooth</u> after a bad storm. Ray wanted
                    11
to go <u>swimming but the lifeguard</u>
                    12
would not let him because <u>there were too many</u> jellyfish in the water.

9 Ⓐ beach. They

Ⓑ beach they.

Ⓒ beach, they

Ⓓ beach they

10 Ⓐ sea shells, driftwood, and even a shark's tooth

Ⓑ sea shells driftwood. And even a shark's tooth

Ⓒ sea shells. Driftwood. And even a shark's tooth

Ⓓ sea shells driftwood and even a shark's tooth

11 Ⓐ swimming but, the lifeguard

Ⓑ swimming, but, the lifeguard

Ⓒ swimming, but the lifeguard

Ⓓ swimming but the lifeguard

12 Ⓐ There were too many

Ⓑ there, were too many

Ⓒ there were, too, many

Ⓓ there were too many

(See page 113 for answer key.)

CHAPTER 7

Language Expression

By the time they are in second grade, most children are becoming eloquent and sophisticated in their ability to express their ideas. They've heard others express themselves and have learned many of the principles they need to handle correct usage, sentences, and paragraphs.

What Your Second Grader Should Be Learning

Your child is now learning to speak quite effectively and correctly. He has learned that our language has both regular and irregular uses, and has learned to generalize language rules. He knows what pronouns are and how to make them possessive. By second grade, most children also learn that some of our more important verbs don't follow regular rules for present and past tense, and they should be ready to learn correct usage of irregular verbs.

But language expression is more than a collection of nouns and verbs. By middle to late second grade, most children are able to understand the building blocks of written expression. They gradually learn that paragraphs are groupings of similar thoughts and they are able to identify what elements belong. They should be able to judge when simple sentences are formed correctly and to pick out incorrect or misplaced elements.

By this age, most children understand the formula of noun-verb-object, such as, "Nancy tossed the ball." Most are able to name where there are mistakes, such as in, "Nancy ball the tossed."

Your child is probably already using the simple tool of reading sentences out loud to determine whether they sound right; if they don't, they are probably formed incorrectly.

What Tests May Ask

Second-grade teachers usually assess how well a child understands the right way to use nouns by grading written essays and by having children fill in blanks or provide short answers to questions.

Unfortunately, current standardized tests assess correct usage through a child's ability to recognize correct usage. These tests typically give a sentence and ask the student to choose the correct answer for the blank. This is much easier for a child than trying to come up with the correct part of speech, possessive, or spelling himself, because all it asks is that he recognize what is right.

What You and Your Child Can Do

By the time your child is in second grade, you should already be doing two important things to teach him language expression: reading to him and talking with him. As you read, you expose him to the words of imaginative writers who communicate in vivid, colorful language. As you continue to read to your child, make sure you choose writers whose styles you and your child enjoy. Choose books that deal with a wide variety of subjects.

Don't stop there. Talk with your children, and expose them to other adults who involve your child in conversation as well. Explain things, such as why you bought a car with side airbags or why you bought a heat pump instead of a conventional heating system. Tell him about your experiences in the military or your childhood memories of summers on your grandparents' farm. Describe how your parents left Poland to escape the Nazis or how your African-American ancestors escaped slavery and obtained an education. Tell him about your job, what you do, and how you care for the family and your home.

Remember that conversation isn't a one-way street; you must also listen to your child. Children at this age are still eager to tell you about their day, how they feel, what they fear, their hopes and dreams, and their opinions. Invite them into conversations when the family gets together. Teach them that you value what they have to say. The attitude that children should be seen and not heard is passé.

Prewriting

Teachers show your child how to "prewrite" as a way of helping them to organize writing. In the old days, "prewriting" really meant outlining; but today teachers have more tools at their disposal, such as block organizing, linear organization, clustering, and mind-mapping. Your second grader isn't too young to learn some of the simpler methods, which will help him learn to organize what he wants to say before he writes it.

Block Organizing

With this method, your child identifies major ideas and then groups lesser ideas under them. Note that a block diagram presents the same information as a traditional outline, but in a way that may make more sense to children. You can easily make your own block organization pages with as many main ideas as necessary, and even expand to multiple pages for longer stories or essays. After they have organized their ideas, children can go block by block to add paragraph by paragraph presentation of their ideas.

Linear Organization

This is another way to visually organize information in which your child uses a left-to-right diagram of the story or essay that allows him to expand beyond main ideas to subordinate ideas, to subsubordinate ideas, and so on, as far to the right as necessary. The left-most entry is the title; ideas for paragraphs go one step to the right; move one step farther to the right for topics within paragraphs.

This system allows your child to organize his ideas before writing a story in final form. However, this method requires your child to choose the most important main ideas first, which is fine if the material has some sequential or chronological order. In situations without a particular order, such as an essay on a favorite TV program, your child will need to think of various reasons for choosing the favorite and the arguments to support each reason.

Clustering

In this method, your child is encouraged to brainstorm, starting with a central idea such as a trip to Florida. (The central idea is usually the same as the title.) Each branch from the central theme links ideas that become the topics for the paragraphs. From there, subtopics branch off, followed by sub-subtopics, and so on. When your child has finished his cluster diagram for a story or essay, it's easy to go back over the diagram to rank paragraphs and then ideas. If he later rejects an idea and all of its subtopics or individual elements, it's easy to cross off individual subcomponents or entire branches during the refinement stage.

Usage

"Usage" simply refers to the correct methods of verbal expression that you can expect of a second grader. At this point, children should know both regular and irregular uses of verb forms, and can learn to generalize language rules.

What Your Child Is Learning

By this age, your child knows that most nouns can be made plural simply by adding an *s*, as in one *toad* and two *toads*. He is able to generalize this rule to include a wide variety of nouns. At the same time, he will become aware that many nouns in our language don't follow this simple rule.

For example, your child may be intrigued by the fact that we see one *man* but that yesterday we saw two *men*. He'll note that one boat is large enough to hold one *family*, while another is large enough to hold several *families*.

Once your child masters simple plurals, in second grade he will move on to understanding how to show possession. Most children this age are able to understand, for example, that most nouns simply require the addition of an apostrophe and an *s* to show possession, such as "Angela's cat" or "the boy's letter." But most second graders won't understand that we show possession of nouns ending in an *s* sound by simply adding an apostrophe, as in "Doris' cat."

Pronouns

Many children at this age find the term "pronoun" confusing, which is why many veteran second-grade teachers are careful to point out that pronouns are simply nouns that stand for other nouns. Children have learned by second grade that:

- *He* is a masculine pronoun.
- *She* is a feminine pronoun.
- *It* is a single neuter item.
- *They* is more than one person, boy, or girl.

In fact, your child may have learned to intentionally misuse pronouns to insult his peers, such as when he refers to a boy as "she," to a girl as "he," or to baby brother or sister as "it."

In second grade, your child will also learn how to use possessive pronouns. For example: "Tyrone took *his* dog to the park, and Jamie took *her* cat to school." Many are a bit confused by the use of "their" and "theirs," such as: "T. J. and Heather took *their* baby brother out to play," and "That book is not ours so it must be *theirs*."

Verb Forms

The correct forms of verbs frequently confuse younger children. Even kindergartners have learned that they can change most verbs to past tense by adding "ed," such as "switched" or "poked." Younger children overgeneralize this rule, such as when your toddler announces, "I *seed* it somewhere."

By second grade, most children become aware that some of the more commonly used verbs don't follow regular rules for present and past tense. *Go* in present tense becomes *went* in the past tense, and *see* in present tense becomes *saw* in past tense. Most second graders begin to learn which common verbs follow regular rules for present and past tense and which verbs are irregular.

Adjectives

Kindergartners and first graders frequently find adjectives confusing. They learn early that they can add "er" or "est" to regular adjectives to describe something as being more or most. But irregular adjectives may confuse them, and they may slip into old habits of overgeneralizing this rule by saying, "One dollar is good, but two dollars are *gooder*."

By second grade, your child should be ready to learn how to use irregular verbs correctly. In the beginning, he'll need to learn the correct forms by rote; but over time, he'll come to recognize correct forms because the incorrect ones won't sound right.

Double Negatives

Kindergartners and many first and second graders continue to use double negatives, such as when Jeffrey announces, "I didn't do nothing," when the teacher questions him crossly. Many children, particularly those who hear double negatives at home or on the playground, may continue to use double negatives in their speech and in their writing. However, by second grade most children are able to understand the logic behind avoiding double negatives.

Paragraphs

In many schools, second grade is the time to introduce the paragraph. Even as late as second grade, many teachers still aren't concerned if students write stories and essays as one long paragraph. Most teachers point out the error to students who divide sentences into paragraphs incorrectly, but they don't grade them harshly for this mistake.

The greatest challenge for young children in dividing written passages into paragraphs is to identify where one paragraph ends and another begins. One way to help figure this out is to be on guard for transitional sentences, as in the following paragraphs:

The first time I met Mr. Carpenter, he was sitting on a chair outside the gas station. He was playing a guitar and singing a song. <u>I remember that he told me that we would meet again. I met Mr. Carpenter again two years later.</u> This time, he knocked on our door and asked my mother if she needed anyone to cut our grass.

What Tests May Ask

In standardized tests for second grade, students are asked to choose the correct noun, verb tense, or pronoun from a list of incorrect choices to fill in a blank. They may also be asked to choose the correct sentence from a group of incorrect choices, or to choose the incorrect choice from a selection of right answers.

Practice Skill: Usage

Directions: Read the following sentences and choose the correct noun to go in the blank.

1 Kathy has a new kitten. Her brother asked their mother, "Did you see _____ new kitten?"

   Ⓐ Kathys

   Ⓑ Kathies

   Ⓒ Kathy's

   Ⓓ Kathyses

2 There was one woman at one table. There were two _____ at the other table.

   Ⓐ womans

   Ⓑ womanses

   Ⓒ women

   Ⓓ woman's

3 The dog was hurt. "Look at that poor _____ paw!" she cried.

   Ⓐ dogs

   Ⓑ dog's

   Ⓒ dogs'

   Ⓓ dogies

4 There were two _____ trotting around the ring.

Ⓐ horse's

Ⓑ horses

Ⓒ horses'

Ⓓ horse

5 Are you going to feed the three _____ some hay?

Ⓐ deers

Ⓑ deers'

Ⓒ deer

Ⓓ deeres

Directions: Read the sentences and choose the correct word to go in the blank.

6 Freddy looked around, but _____ could not find Charlie.

Ⓐ he

Ⓑ him

Ⓒ his

Ⓓ it

7 Linda bought a birthday card for _____ best friend Jay.

Ⓐ Jay

Ⓑ its

Ⓒ her

Ⓓ she

8 Fiona ran to jump on _____ sled.

Ⓐ she

Ⓑ his

Ⓒ her

Ⓓ its

Directions: Choose the sentence that is written correctly.

9 Ⓐ Tracey goed to her friend's house.

Ⓑ Terri seen his dog Sparky run down the street.

Ⓒ Chris went to the movies.

Ⓓ Barbara and Jamie sees their grandmother every Sunday.

Directions: Choose the correct verb to go in the blank in this sentence.

10 Alma _____ to throw the ball through the hoop, but she missed.

Ⓐ tryed

Ⓑ try

Ⓒ tried

Ⓓ tryded

Directions: Choose the sentence that is written correctly.

11 Ⓐ Vanilla ice cream is good, but strawberry is better. I like chocolate best of all.

Ⓑ Kara is the goodest skater on our team.

Ⓒ John is fast, and Bill is faster, but Sally is the faster of them all.

Ⓓ I think my dog Buffy is smartest than Sam's dog Poochie.

12 Ⓐ It is coldest today than it was yesterday.

Ⓑ The apple pie is gooder than the peach pie.

Ⓒ My grandmother is older than my grandfather.

Ⓓ She is nicest than her sister.

Directions: Choose the INCORRECT sentence.

13 Ⓐ Jimmy did not lose his book.

Ⓑ Anna never saw no deer.

Ⓒ Maria has never been to Springfield.

Ⓓ Mr. Gannet will not be able to go on the trip.

Directions: Choose the sentence that is written correctly.

14 Ⓐ Sam ball the took.

Ⓑ Pool in Sara swam the.

Ⓒ I think the pretty blue is dress.

Ⓓ My birthday is tomorrow.

15 Ⓐ Did Jeffrey call mother his?

Ⓑ What time is over class?

Ⓒ Oh, I spilled my milk.

Ⓓ Justin song the sang.

(See page 113 for answer key.)

CHAPTER 8

Spelling

In the adult world, your child will be judged based on his use of correct or incorrect spelling. Even former vice presidents pay a heavy price for misspelling words like "potato." This fact makes it puzzling that so many adults proudly proclaim that they can't spell.

In recent years, many teachers have spent less time emphasizing spelling than they did in the past. Many elementary schools have misapplied the concept of invented spelling (which simply encourages separating the teaching of writing and spelling in the early grades) to ignore the importance of correct spelling at all. The correct use of invented spelling encourages beginning writers to learn to express their ideas in writing without experiencing unduly harsh criticism and punishment for misspellings, concentrating instead on learning how to properly use nouns, verbs, and the other elements of the sentence and the paragraph.

However, the use of invented spelling doesn't mean you shouldn't teach spelling as a separate activity and gradually require students to incorporate correct spelling into their writing as they become more secure. Unfortunately, in many elementary classrooms across the country, teachers have abandoned teaching spelling altogether.

What Your Second Grader Should Be Learning

Most children who have received proper spelling instruction in first grade are ready by second grade to apply these principles to spell common words. For example, when your child hears the word "cat," she should be able to predict that the first letter is either a "c" or a "k" and that the remaining sounds will be made with "a" followed by "t."

Most have learned common single- and double-syllable words in first grade, and by second grade are ready to begin learning some of the more common irregularly spelled words, such as "women" and "nation." Your child should also be ready to learn common spelling rules, such as "*i* before *e*, except after *c*, or when sounded as *a*, as in *neighbor* and *weigh*." Expect your second grader to incorporate more multisyllable and irregularly spelled words into her spelling repertoire.

Most second graders begin to appreciate that American English is a conglomeration of many different languages, each with its own spelling and pronunciation rules. For example, we use the Icelandic word *tyke* (which literally means *female dog* in that language) to refer to a small child. In the Deep South, we use the Algonquin word *Yankee* (which literally means *rude or classless person*) to refer to individuals from the North. The nature of our language is such that any given sentence may be composed from words of any of a number of combinations in derivation, such as German, Latin, French, and Italian.

If your child has received proper spelling instruction in first grade, she'll also be able to begin to edit for spelling errors. She will be able to look over her writing and note words she knows are misspelled and flag suspicious words, and to look them up in the dictionary.

What You and Your Child Can Do

One veteran teacher approaches spelling using word groups. For example, one week she teaches a unit on fruit words and asks her students to bring in pictures of peaches or cherries to put on a bulletin board with the correct spelling underneath. Her students sample blueberry jam, and the class makes grape juice and visits a nearby apple orchard, where they sample apples, applesauce, and apple juice and watch how the workers process the apples they pick. In another unit, she emphasizes -ade words, and she brings in a garden *spade*, the children make *lemonade*, and her husband *Wade* pays a visit. She manages to teach a word unit per week, and her students progress to use correct spelling in their writing eagerly, never feeling ridiculed or punished by the approach.

Take a cue from such veteran teachers and gently teach spelling at home. In early first grade, begin by separating writing and spelling. Concentrate on helping your child learn to express herself properly in writing and, separately, begin to build her spelling repertoire. If your child is interested in zoo animals, make out word cards for *gorilla* and *tiger* and other zoo animal names and drill her on the spellings. If she is interested in ships, make out cards for words such as *keel*, *anchor*, and *sail*. Gradually begin to point out words, especially words your child has studied in spelling, both when she spells them correctly and when she spells them incorrectly.

Edit Your Child's Work. By second grade, children should become more accustomed to the process of editing. When your beginning second grader writes a note to Aunt Barbara thanking her for the sweater, have her write a rough draft (or "sloppy copy") and then go over it with her

for glaring errors. If you detect a misspelled word, see if she can furnish the correct spelling.

Look It Up. Show your child how to look up a word in an age-appropriate dictionary. If the word isn't in a child's dictionary, use another dictionary aimed at below-college level.

Homework Checks. Use the same strategy with homework. By the time she is in middle second grade, you should go over your child's written homework and point out misspellings. Be prepared for some teachers to resist your efforts at correcting your child's spelling. It's important that you help your child get used to having her written work edited. The longer we allow children to practice incorrect spelling, the more difficult it will be for them to learn the correct way.

As you edit your child's homework and the school papers she brings home, make a list of words your child routinely misspells. You'll find your child will routinely misspell the same words and make the same errors (usually one or two letters) in each difficult word. Make note cards with those words, with the routinely misspelled letters CAPITALIZED, and drill her on the challenging words from time to time. For example, if she routinely misspells the word *school* as "skool," write it on the note card as "sCHool."

Most state departments of public instruction provide lists of required (or recommended) words that children at each grade level should be able to read and spell. These lists can be a helpful resource because they are generally designed to match the vocabulary children in each grade encounter in the curriculum, and the level of vocabulary tested in the standardized tests each state uses.

Word Lists. Ask your child's teacher for a copy of your state's second grade word list. If your teacher can't provide this, write to the instructional division of your state department of public instruction to ask whether there is a list and how you can obtain a copy.

Flash Cards. Make flash cards and drill your child on the words. When your child spells a word correctly, give her immediate feedback with a cue, such as "Right!" or "Good!" If the spelling is incorrect, say "No" and immediately correct her, either by spelling the word correctly or by showing the flash card answer and spelling it aloud. Have your child spell it correctly before moving on to the next word.

Spelling Software. Look for grade-appropriate software, such as *Spelling Blaster*. These programs provide immediate feedback and have the added advantage of presenting spelling in a non-threatening, fun video game format that most children enjoy. If your child wants to use the family computer, visit the school and check out their software; obtain the same software, if possible.

If your second grader enjoys using your adult word processing software, turn on automatic spell flagging to help provide immediate feedback. New adult-level word processing software provides alerts such as alarm buzzes, flashing red underlines, or other ways of noting misspelled words. Although these programs flag words that they simply don't recognize (such as many proper names), they also flag misspellings, such as when a child writes, "I road the *buse* to school." (But note that they would typically not flag the incorrect spelling of "road" because that is a correct spelling in another context.)

What Tests May Ask

Standardized testing of spelling can't ask your child to come up with her own spelling; she will be asked to choose the correct spelling from a list of incorrect choices, or to choose the one incorrect word from a list of possibilities. Tests typically include difficult words that require a child to recognize the irregular use of spelling sounds, such as "*sch*" to make the "*sk*" sound.

Practice Skill: Spelling

Directions: Choose the correctly spelled word to go into the blank.

1 I picked an _____ off the tree in my backyard.
   Ⓐ appul
   Ⓑ apul
   Ⓒ appel
   Ⓓ apple

2 Lana is a girl I met at ____.
   Ⓐ school
   Ⓑ skool
   Ⓒ skul
   Ⓓ skule

3 Tommy is my _____. We do lots of things together.
   Ⓐ freend
   Ⓑ friend
   Ⓒ frend
   Ⓓ frende

4 I like to _____ my own clothes.
   Ⓐ chose
   Ⓑ choose
   Ⓒ choise
   Ⓓ chuge

Directions: Pick out the word that is spelled INCORRECTLY in this sentence.

5 Kristi loved to run down to the grade schule every morning.

Ⓐ morning

Ⓑ schule

Ⓒ loved

Ⓓ run

6 I just know that today I'm going to receive a wonderful suprise.

Ⓐ today

Ⓑ receive

Ⓒ suprise

Ⓓ know

(See page 113 for answer key.)

CHAPTER 9

Math Concepts

In many curricula, second grade mathematics is primarily a review of concepts taught in first grade. But second grade is also a time when children begin to see that there is an order in mathematics that is consistent and predictable if we only learn the principles involved. They see that there is more to the universe of mathematics than simply counting what is there, and they also learn how they can use math in their lives.

What Your Second Grader Should Be Learning

Second graders begin to be able to visualize the relationship between mathematics, objects in space, and three-dimensional movement. They begin to spell out numbers, although most still do not understand the complex rules for when it is correct to spell out a number and when it is correct to express it numerically. By middle second grade, they should be comfortable with numbers from 0 to 100 and above, and should accurately identify all multiples of 10 up to 100. They should also be able to accurately identify all numerals in between, such as 47, 68, and 93.

Your child should be comfortable with the concepts of "more than" and "less than." By the end of second grade, he will be able to accurately answer simple number sentences with the symbols, including addition, subtraction, and greater than or less than. He'll be able to round and estimate, skip count, identify fraction parts, and solve number sentences.

What You Can Do

First, accept one basic assumption: No matter how bright your child is, there is no way to avoid rote memorization and practice in learning math concepts. We can try to make the process as painless and as child-friendly as possible, but we only learn math concepts when we make a focused effort to learn them and set aside time to practice them.

Math Notebook

Create a math notebook to keep at home for your second grader, with a divider for each chapter in the textbook, and more dividers for concepts and terminology and any other sections that make sense.

When math papers come home, file them under the corresponding chapter in the text, along with any homework your child brings home. (Some teachers require children to maintain folders at school with this work. In this case, instead of filing papers at home, note in each chapter what problems your child encountered.)

Whenever your child encounters a new concept, make an entry in the "concepts" section of the notebook. From time to time, go back and drill your child on concepts that were presented earlier to make sure that even ideas he's not working on in class remain fresh. Each time you encounter a new term or symbol that your child hasn't had before, write it down under the "terminology" section and make a flash card for it. Keep the flash cards with the terminology and occasionally play flash cards.

Make sure that your child masters the fundamentals of all math concepts taught in earlier grades. If your child was introduced to the number line in kindergarten, for example, return to the number line occasionally to make sure that your child hasn't forgotten this skill.

Math in Action!

Explain how you use mathematics every day and why you do what you do. Explain the concepts involved. If you enjoy photography, show your second grader how you calculate the length of exposure and why some films require longer exposure times than others. If your child likes model rocketry, show him how to calculate trajectory, flight time, and drift.

Check for Errors

Look over your child's math homework to see if there are any consistent error patterns. For example, if your child consistently makes subtraction mistakes in problems that require regrouping, make up drill sheets and flash cards of problems requiring regrouping. Drill until your child reaches near 100 percent accuracy.

Math Software

Look for some of the new educational software programs that deal in math, such as *Math Blaster*. Today, software incorporates fascinating sounds, colorful pictures, talking characters, and games that make math fascinating and fun. The better instructional programs even keep a running record for each user, noting where he consistently makes mistakes so the program can tailor lessons and remedial activities to the user's needs.

Numeration

Until second grade, children have been accustomed to writing numbers as numerals (1, 2, 3). In second grade, most schools begin to introduce numbers expressed as words (one, two, three). Second graders learn first to spell the words for the numerals 1 through 10, then zero, and by the end of second grade, multiples of 10, such as twenty through one hundred.

Recognizing Numerals 0 to 100

Your child probably began learning how to recognize numerals up to 100 during first grade, although understanding of numerals past 10 may have been weak. In early second grade, most schools begin to emphasize more accurate and automatic recognition of numerals up to 100; at this point, most children should have progressed beyond identifying 21 as "eleventeen" and 110 as "eleventy." By middle second grade, your child should be able to accurately identify all multiples of 10 up to 100 and all numerals in between, such as 47, 68, and 93.

Recognizing Numerals Above 100

Many schools then progress to recognition of numerals above 100, and teach the principles that will allow children to identify numerals they see up to one million. By the end of second grade, most children are able to identify even larger numerals with great accuracy.

Practice Skill: Numeration

Directions: Read the following questions and select the correct answer.

1 Choose the word for the number <u>30</u>.

Ⓐ twenty

Ⓑ thirty

Ⓒ thirteen

Ⓓ threty

2 Which number means 4 tens and 6 ones?

Ⓐ 4060   Ⓑ 0406

Ⓒ 46   Ⓓ 406

3 Choose the names of the words for 7,142.

(A) seventy thousand, one hundred, and forty-two

(B) seven point one four two

(C) seventy-one thousand and two-two

(D) seven thousand, one hundred, and forty-two

4 Choose the number that tells what we have if we have two groups of one thousand plus six groups of one hundred plus nine.

(A) 26,1009

(B) 2.690

(C) 260,009

(D) 2,609

(See pages 113–114 for answer key.)

Number Concepts

Even most toddlers are able to see a beach ball and a golf ball and state that the first is bigger than the second. By the time they are in kindergarten and first grade, most children are able to see a box with a few buttons on one side of a table and state that it has fewer buttons than one on the other side of the table that has hundreds of buttons, even if the boxes are not the same size.

Comparing and Ordering Whole Numbers

By the time they are in second grade, most children are ready to become stronger and more automatic in comparing whole numbers and are able to state relationships such as *more*, *fewer*, and *same*. These are important concepts that are covered by standardized tests as well.

They'll learn this concept first with single dig-its, learning that 9 is always greater than 6, for example. But they will also learn the converse: If 9 is greater than 6, then 6 is less than 9. As they progress to numbers with more than one digit, they will learn that, with whole, positive numbers, the number with the most digits is always greater than the number with fewer digits. In multidigit numbers with the same number of digits, the number whose left-most digit is the greatest is always the greatest number. If the left-most digits in two numbers are the same, they must work one digit at a time to the right to determine the greater number.

Once they are secure in the ability to determine more than, less than, and equal to relationships, children begin to be able to order values. They will learn ordering in their own minor purchases. For example, if they find that Store A sells Captain Moonbeam card packs for $3, Store B sells them for $2, and Store C sells them for $4, they will learn that they first need to try Store B, then Store A, and only if neither of those has them, Store C. (That is, Store B is their first choice, Store A their second choice, and Store C their last choice.)

Recognizing and Solving Number Sentences

Until second grade, most math curricula present math problems vertically, such as:

$$\begin{array}{r} 12 \\ +3 \\ \hline 15 \end{array}$$

By second grade, most schools begin to introduce number sentences, which are sometimes called expressions. Number sentences are simply mathematical expressions presented in linear form, such as:

$$5 + 6 = 11$$

By late second grade, children are familiar with a few mathematical symbols, such as addition (+), subtraction (−), equality (=), less than (<), greater than (>), less than or equal to (≤), greater than or equal to (≥), and does not equal (≠). Most late second graders have learned to read from left to right, so that the expression in the previous example is read as "five plus six equals eleven."

Identifying Fractional Parts

Most second-grade teachers introduce the number of fractional parts but don't yet emphasize complex fractions. Depending on the school, these typically come in fourth or fifth grade. But even by second grade, most children are able to understand that if there are four people splitting a pizza, it should be cut into four equal parts. Most second-grade math classes introduce fractions so that children can start thinking about them.

Determining Ordinal Position

As children become more familiar with counting, numerical relationships, ordering, and values, they become familiar with differences in ordinal positions. Even young toddlers learn what it means to shout, "Me first!" and barge to the front of a line.

By second grade, most schools begin to emphasize designation of ordinal positions, so by late in the school year most students have learned the principles behind adding the suffixes that make *thirteen* into *thirteenth*, *thirty-three* into *thirty-third*, and so on.

Rounding and Estimating

Think back to when your second grader was a toddler and then a preschooler, and you will probably recall a very rigid little person. If Big Sister pointed out that what the family saw swoop down to the lake and snatch up a fish was an eagle, little Janey would insist, "It's not an eagle, it's a bird." When 4-year-old Jeffrey was told his cousin is 4 years old, he would insist, "She can't be 4, I'm 4!"

As your child becomes more comfortable with numerical concepts, and as his reasoning powers become more flexible, he will begin to understand the concept of rounding. When Mother pays $1.49 for a gallon of gas and tells Dad, "I had to pay a dollar and a half for gas," younger children will insist that she only paid $1.49.

Initially, your child may more readily understand rounding when the fractional part of a number is only slightly above the integer to which it is rounded, such as when the cereal costs $2.02 or the plank is 3 feet 1 inch long and the values are rounded to $2 and 3 feet, respectively. Gradually, he will learn the rules of rounding, so that if the fractional value is less than half, we round down, and if it is half or more, we round up.

Once he is comfortable with rounding, the concept of estimation is only a short step away. If your child needs a board 2 feet long for his dog house, but he doesn't have a tape measure handy, he will be able to go to the lumber stack and pick out one that is probably long enough.

Counting Using Groups of 10

One of the earliest patterns children learn is counting by tens because they have 10 fingers and can generalize from groups of 10 fingers to the concept of counting 10, 20, 30. The ability to count in groups is a precursor to a skill that in third or fourth grade will become the ability to multiply. For now, be content that your second grader can understand counting using groups of 10.

Skip Counting

Closely related to the ability to count using groups of 10 is the ability to generalize that skill to groups of other numbers. For example, children at this age learn that they can count by twos (2, 4, 6, 8), threes (3, 6, 9), fours (4, 8, 12), and fives (5, 10, 15). By the end of second grade, most will be able to skip count by 2, 3, 4, 5, and multiples of 10, 100, and 1000.

Understanding Place Value

The concept of place value is a fairly sophisticated one and gives many children difficulty throughout their elementary school careers. The realization that the number 621 indicates six groups of one hundred, two groups of ten, and one group of one, for example, eludes many children. Even by late second grade, most children are limited to understanding place values up to three.

Practice Skill: Number Concepts

Directions: Read the following questions and choose the correct response.

5 Which team has the <u>fewest</u> players?

 Ⓐ

 Ⓑ

 Ⓒ

 Ⓓ

6 James and his twin brother John helped pick up trash on the side of the road in front of their home. James picked up 11 pounds of trash, and John picked up 14 pounds of trash. Choose the correct sentence:

Ⓐ James picked up more trash than John did.

Ⓑ John picked up more trash than James did.

Ⓒ James and John picked up the same amount of trash.

Ⓓ John and James picked up the same amount of trash.

7 Choose the numbers that are in the correct order from least to most:

Ⓐ 12, 15, 18, 11

Ⓑ 11, 14, 19, 17

Ⓒ 6, 4, 2, 1

Ⓓ 10, 20, 99, 100

Directions: Read these number sentences and choose the correct answer that goes in the blank.

8 60 + 12 = ___

Ⓐ 62

Ⓑ 6012

Ⓒ 48

Ⓓ 72

9 8 + ___ = 12

(A) 128

(B) 4

(C) 20

(D) 812

10 5 + 7 = ___

(A) 6 + 6

(B) 4 + 9

(C) 15 −12

(D) 3 + 10

11 Lisa, Jimmy, and Michael baked a cherry pie. Lisa said, "This pie is not very big, but it will be big enough for all of us to share." Which picture shows how Lisa, Jimmy, and Michael should cut the pie so that they will each get the same amount of pie?

(A)   (B)

(C)   (D)

12 Which animal is <u>fourth</u> in line for tickets?

(A) rooster

(B) lion

(C) goat

(D) dog

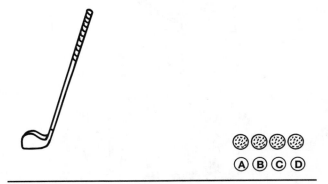

13 Which ball is <u>fourth</u> from the golf club?

Directions: Round these numbers to their nearest whole number.

14 $3\frac{1}{8}$

(A) 3

(B) 4

(C) 1

(D) 8

15 $59^{1}/_{2}$

Ⓐ 59

Ⓑ 2

Ⓒ 60

Ⓓ 1

16 About where is the ball on the football field?

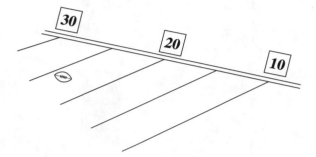

Ⓐ 20 yard line

Ⓑ 24 yard line

Ⓒ 30 yard line

Ⓓ 34 yard line

17 Melinda broke one of her pencils. About how much of the broken pencil is left?

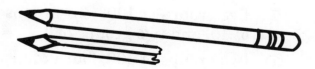

Ⓐ none of it

Ⓑ all of it

Ⓒ about half of it

Ⓓ about one and one-half of it

18 Jean and Sam work on their parents' farm putting apples into bags to sell at the grocery store. Each bag holds 10 apples. If their father tells them he needs them to fill 4 bags, how many apples do they need to put in the bags in all?

Ⓐ 20

Ⓑ 40

Ⓒ 60

Ⓓ 4

19 We are going to count by threes. Choose the number to fill in the blank in this series of numbers: 12, 15, 18, ___, 24, 27

Ⓐ 21

Ⓑ 19

Ⓒ 20

Ⓓ 23

20 Donna sold tickets at her school for the hot dog supper for $5.00 each. After the supper, her mother helped her count how much money she had collected. She counted the $5 bills: $5, $10, $15, $20, __, $30, $35. What number goes in the blank?

Ⓐ $15

Ⓑ $21

Ⓒ $27

Ⓓ $25

21 Look at the pattern in the figure below. Choose the clock that would come next.

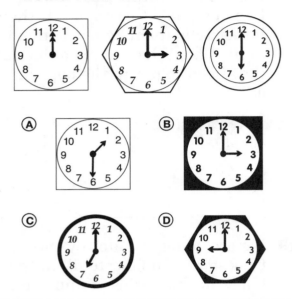

22 Look at the pattern in the picture below. Choose the picture that should come next.

23 Look at the picture below. Which card goes next?

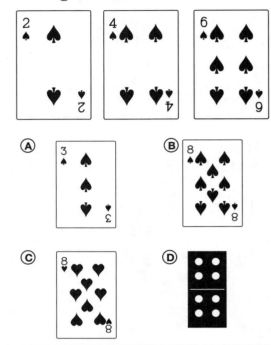

24 Choose the number that shows seven groups of 100, 9 groups of 10, and no groups of 1.

  Ⓐ 970   Ⓑ 700900

  Ⓒ 777990   Ⓓ 790

25 Which answer below tells the value of 542?

  Ⓐ five groups of 100, four groups of 10, and two groups of 1

  Ⓑ two groups of 100, four groups of 10, and five groups of one

  Ⓒ five groups of 1000, four groups of 100, and 2 groups of 10

  Ⓓ None of these answers tells the value of 542.

(See pages 113–114 for answer key.)

Properties

Using a Number Line

Some schools introduce the number line as early as kindergarten, while others introduce it as late as second grade, if at all. Particularly if your child's school uses either a very old or a very new curriculum, you'll be introduced to the number line, such as this one:

1 2 3 4 5 6 7 8 9 10 11 12 13 14 15 16 17 18 19 20

Note that, in second grade, children aren't yet familiar with the concept of negative numbers. In fact, that will come much later. Children are generally not yet familiar with fractions (such as 5 1/2) or decimals beyond money values (such as 5.5). Instead, they concentrate on whole numbers, also called integers. Teachers introduce the number line this way: If we wish to add 4 and 3, we refer to the following number line:

$\downarrow$

1 2 3 4 5 6 7 8 9 10 11 12 13 14 15 16 17 18 19 20

We then move three counts to the <u>right</u>, in this manner:

$\downarrow \rightarrow \downarrow$

1 2 3 4 5 6 7 8 9 10 11 12 13 14 15 16 17 18 19 20

The important concept that children are learning with the number line at this stage is that to add, we move to the right, while to subtract, we move to the left. (You will see the number line again in late junior high or early high school when your child begins pre-algebra and must become familiar with negative numbers and operations using them.)

Using Expanded Notation

We have touched on expanded notation in the descriptions of operations that are new to sec-

ond graders. But, by the end of second grade, most children are more comfortable and automatic in discriminating one mathematical symbol from another and in automatically applying the correct mathematical operation it calls for.

Using Operational Symbols and Properties

Even though second graders often review math concepts learned in first grade, by late second grade most children are able to integrate the concepts they first saw in first grade with the new concepts. They are also much stronger and automatic in applying the concepts learned, even to the extent of being able to perform some mixed operations, such as:

$$7 - 6 + 9 - 2 = 8$$

Understanding Terminology

The operations we have introduced thus far in this chapter bring with them new terms for your second grader, which may also appear on standardized tests. This year in school, they will learn terms such as:

borrowing

equivalent

estimate, estimation

fraction

greater than

grouping

integer

less than

not equal to

number line

regrouping

skip counting

Practice Skill: Properties

Directions: Choose the correct symbols to fill in the blanks for these math problems.

26 2 _____ 3 = 5

Ⓐ —

Ⓑ +

Ⓒ ×

Ⓓ =

27 9 ___ 5

Ⓐ <

Ⓑ =

Ⓒ >

Ⓓ +

28 8 __ 7 = 1

Ⓐ <

Ⓑ >

Ⓒ —

Ⓓ +

29 Choose the correct answer to go in the blank in this problem:
12 − 4 − 4 = ___

Ⓐ 8

Ⓑ 16

Ⓒ 4

Ⓓ 20

30 What is another way of saying that 8 is less than 12?

Ⓐ 8 > 12

Ⓑ 8 < 12

Ⓒ 8 { 12

Ⓓ 8 % 12

31 Choose the group in which the numbers inside the triangles are <u>greater than</u> the numbers inside the squares:

Ⓐ

15   9

5   9

Ⓑ

4   5

5   4

Ⓒ

30   90

40   100

Ⓓ

3   4

1   2

32 <u>Estimate</u> the length of the piece of string.

```
| 1  2  3  4  5  6
```

Ⓐ exactly 4 inches long

Ⓑ exactly 5 inches long

Ⓒ about 4 inches long

Ⓓ about 5 inches long

(See pages 113–114 for answer key.)

CHAPTER 10

Math Computation

To a great extent, second grade math is a review and reinforcement of the mathematics principles taught in first grade. Functions that your first grader would struggle to perform, stopping to count on fingers, will become more accurate, quick, and automatic in second grade.

What Your Second Grader Should Be Learning

By the end of second grade, most children should be able to add and subtract one-, two-, and three-digit numbers with regrouping. Although most second graders are able to see the relationship between multiplication and addition problems, the concept of adapting division problems to subtraction is beyond most second graders.

What Tests May Ask

Tests at second grade may ask your child to perform vertical addition and subtraction tasks using one, two, or three numbers. Children need to choose the correct answer from a group of possible choices. When faced with linear addition problems such as:

$$542 + 389 = 931$$

children should learn to rewrite the problem as:

$$\begin{array}{r} 542 \\ +389 \\ \hline 931 \end{array}$$

What You and Your Child Can Do

Second-grade teachers say that simple, careless mistakes rob children of 20 percent of their math grades. Perhaps Jeffrey carelessly adds 6 plus 6 and gets 66 or Shara subtracts 12 from 23 and gets 35. While there are fun activities to increase your child's accuracy and interest in math computation, there is no substitution for rote memorization and practice in overcoming careless errors.

If you're keeping the math notebook recommended in Chapter 9 and you're carefully studying the math papers and assignments your child brings home, you already know a lot about which skills you need to reinforce.

Use Flash Cards. For every new operation, make up flash cards with problems like those your child has in school. Set aside a time each day to work with your child. Don't forget to include flash cards with problems on them using skills she's previously learned. Drill them at odd moments (while at traffic lights, in the doctor's office, and so on). Drill them until they become fast, automatic, and accurate.

Neatness Counts. Make sure your child writes legibly. If no one can read her answers, she can't get credit for them. If your child writes illegibly, have her write out a rough draft of her math homework and copy it over before she hands it in. Check out how your child writes numbers: They should all stand out sharply so that anyone can identify them. If she has problems with specific numbers, have her practice writing them in a standard way until she writes them nearly perfectly. Compliment her when you see neatness and legibility.

Graph It! Make sure your child aligns columns appropriately. If she has problems with alignment, buy graph paper with squares large enough to write one numeral per square, and let her use it for her rough drafts. Sometimes children simply don't know that they're supposed to line up their problems. Show them. Then show them how proper alignment allows them to be sure which number is added to or subtracted from another. As you look over their work, point out misalignments. If this is a common problem for your child, talk with her teacher and get permission to send graph paper for her to use in class.

Copy Accurately. Make sure your child copies problems correctly. Many an evening has been spent with a child crying and Mom or Dad yelling, frustrated that they can't make the problem come out with the answer in the key in the back of the book, only to find out that the child didn't copy the problem correctly. Look over her homework and make sure she transfers the problems correctly from her textbook to her paper. Have her check every word and every number. If there are figures such as geometric designs, make sure she copies them correctly.

If this is a problem at home, it's almost certainly a problem at school, where transferring from the chalkboard to the paper is even more difficult than transferring from the book to the paper.

Use a Calculator. Teach your child how to check over problems with a calculator. Use this aid for homework only, to check answers, never to calculate answers.

Play Computer Games. The new crop of mathematics software often pinpoints where children make frequent errors and provide games, flash card exercises, and other drills to reinforce and automate computation skills. Look over the selection of age- or grade-appropriate math instruc-

tion programs. Read the blurbs on the boxes to determine whether the programs emphasize the skills your child needs. Ask your child's teacher to recommend appropriate programs.

Addition

By the end of second grade, most children should be able to add one-, two-, and three-digit numbers with regrouping (sometimes called "carrying" or "carrying over") in vertical format, such as:

$$312$$
$$+469$$
$$781$$

Note that the above example requires carrying over the 10 from adding 2 + 9 in the ones column, so that, instead of adding 10 + 60 in the middle column, we are adding 20 + 60. Many children struggle with this concept at first, but by the end of second grade, most are stronger and more automatic. They will be ready, in third grade, to move to adding more rows of numbers and to adding numbers with more columns.

Practice Skill: Addition

Directions: Select the correct answers to these problems.

1   395
    +395

Ⓐ 790

Ⓑ 680

Ⓒ 780

Ⓓ 690

2 117
+225

   Ⓐ 3312

   Ⓑ 332

   Ⓒ 442

   Ⓓ 342

(See page 114 for answer key.)

Subtraction

In first grade your child learned some subtraction, but she probably won't become proficient at subtracting even single-digit numbers until second grade.

Subtracting Whole Numbers

By the end of second grade, most children are quite competent at subtraction, even when it requires regrouping up to three digits and across zeros. For example,

   307
 −258
    49

As with addition, when faced with linear subtraction problems, such as

$$307 - 258 = 49$$

your child will find it necessary to rewrite the problem in the margin in vertical form, as:

   307
 −258
    49

Practice Skill: Subtraction

Directions: Choose the correct answers to each of these problems.

3 200
−77

   Ⓐ 277

   Ⓑ 123

   Ⓒ 233

   Ⓓ 203

4 520
−60

   Ⓐ 477

   Ⓑ 460

   Ⓒ 230

   Ⓓ 210

(See page 114 for answer key.)

Multiplication

Not until third or fourth grade will children become competent in what we normally think of as multiplication. Now, your child can set the stage for later competency in multiplication by extending some of the concepts she's already learned. For example:

Sam and Kara each bought a box of Fruit Wackies with 20 candies in each box. How many candies did they have in all?

Although your older child would know to form this problem as a multiplication problem expressed as:

$$20$$
$$\times 2$$
$$\overline{40}$$

your second grader will learn to form the problem as an addition problem:

$$20$$
$$+20$$
$$\overline{40}$$

Such problem transformation will help children understand later that multiplication is an extension of addition. They'll see the efficiency of multiplication over addition, especially when the number of items they must multiply increases, such as in this problem:

Jake wanted to play football for the Midtown Pee Wee League, so he began running. He ran 14 laps around the track each day for 19 days. How many laps did he run in all?

By the time your child will actually be faced with such problems in third or fourth grade, she will see that she can set up the problem as adding 19 rows of 14, but it's more efficient to set up the problem as:

$$14$$
$$\times 19$$
$$\overline{266}$$

For now, be content for her to set up multiplication situations as addition.

Practice Skill: Multiplication

Directions: Select the correct answers to the following questions.

5 Donna and Jim each bought a pack of notebook paper at the school store. Each pack had 25 sheets of paper. How many sheets of paper did they have altogether?

- (A) 2525
- (B) 50
- (C) 250
- (D) 120

6 Baxter, Bob, and Sparky are puppies. Their boy Ron wanted to give each of them three puppy treats. How many puppy treats does he need to take out of the pack?

- (A) 8
- (B) 10
- (C) 9
- (D) 12

(See page 114 for answer key.)

Division

Although most second graders are able to adapt multiplication scenarios to addition problems, the concept of adapting division problems to subtraction causes most children more difficulty. For example, when confronted with the following problem:

T. J.'s class was going on a field trip. There were 24 children, and 6 parents had agreed to drive. How many children will be in each car if each car holds the same number of children?

Even many second graders have trouble understanding that they can set up the problem by seeing how many times they can subtract 6 from 24.

Don't worry if your child still doesn't understand this concept by the end of second grade. This skill usually develops after the ability to convert multiplication problems to addition. Often, children don't develop this ability until third or fourth grade. Nevertheless, there may be some questions on standardized tests that assess understanding of this concept.

Practice Skill: Division

Directions: Read the following questions and choose the correct answer.

7 Elise, Millie, and Elaine baked cookies one rainy day. They baked 12 cookies. If they divided them equally among themselves, how many cookies did each child receive?

Ⓐ 4
Ⓑ 15
Ⓒ 5
Ⓓ 6

8 Jake picked 18 apples. His grandmother gave him 3 baskets to hold the apples. If he put the same number of apples in each basket, how many apples did he put in each basket?

Ⓐ 15
Ⓑ 6
Ⓒ 21
Ⓓ 12

(See page 114 for answer key.)

CHAPTER 11

Math Applications

The field of behavior modification relies very heavily on a principal called *Grandma's Rule*: "First eat your peas and carrots, and then you get dessert." Now that we've progressed beyond the drills, memorization, and rote learning of the preceding two chapters, it's time for some fun. This chapter presents the dessert part of math: specific applications.

The ability to apply elementary mathematics skills to all sorts of fun and useful activities distinguishes second graders from their younger peers. This can be an exciting time for your child, when he can begin to explore many new and fascinating areas. And yet these practical areas—measuring, time, calendars, graphs, and charts—also appear on standardized tests.

What Your Second Grader Should Be Learning

By the end of second grade, most children have a quick, accurate, and automatic grasp of hours, minutes, seconds, days, weeks, months, and years. However, most second graders still have some problems performing mixed calculations, such as using a combination of days, hours, or minutes or of years, months, and days.

By late second grade, many children are able to make general estimates of temperature—warm (the 70s), cold (the 20s or 30s), and very hot (above 200) conditions—but are not able to make precise estimates in between.

When it comes to geometry, most second graders have a general understanding of geometric shapes, but don't expect your second grader to understand the process of finding perimeters of circular or curved figures. That, and even more complex operations, will come later.

What Tests May Ask

Standardized tests at the second-grade level ask your child to find perimeters, match shapes, and make choices indicating an understanding of spatial relationships. They also assess your child's ability to estimate and to measure, and answer questions about time, weight, and size. In addition, the tests present word problems in a way that will assess your child's underlying skill and his ability to set up the problem and understand what it's asking.

What You and Your Child Can Do

If your child is to do well on standardized math tests, he must feel comfortable and competent in math. Your child will respond better to a positive attitude toward math that he sees in your behavior on a daily basis than he will to some verbal claim that math is a good thing, especially if you're obviously math phobic yourself and proud of it. Many adults who would be offended if someone accused them of being illiterate proudly lament that they can't balance a checkbook or set the time on a VCR. If your child *sees* that you are afraid of or don't value math, then nothing you *say* will encourage him to enjoy it.

If you doubt your own abilities in math, now is an excellent time to overcome that fear: Check out books from the library on how to strengthen your math. Take remedial courses at the local adult school or buy math review computer programs. Let your child *see* you value math.

Translate Abstract Ideas into Concrete. One of the biggest problems second graders have is translating the abstract into the concrete. If your child has trouble with word problems (Nora had 4 guppies. One of the guppies had 10 babies. How many guppies did Nora have then?), open a bag of beans and pretend that each bean is a guppy. Start with 4 bean guppies and then add 10 more "babies." Then count them.

Models also help children understand some scenarios. Sugar cubes, alphabet blocks, Legos, and other materials allow children to build models that copy a problem and simply count the blocks.

Make a Counting Tool. Egyptian teachers used stringing beads to help their students count thousands of years ago. It's a method that still works today. Make a counting rod by substituting a narrow dowel mounted vertically or horizontally to accomplish the same purpose. Or buy a high-quality abacus at an educational supply store, and let your child help you learn how to use it.

Make a Counting Board. You can make a counting board from a 4-foot × 4-foot piece of pegboard from a local builder's supply store. Use string and pegs, for example, to teach graphing.

Travel. Visit educational attractions such as zoos, aquariums, planetariums, and children's museums that teach mathematics in a fun, hands-on way.

On the Job. If your job or your hobbies involve mathematics, share that with your child. It's not important that he understands the operations involved, but that he understands that math is important. If you enjoy photography as a hobby, show him the math involved: the focal length of lenses, the ISO ratings of films, *f*-stops, shutter speeds, and so on.

Music Lessons. If it's at all possible within your budget, and if your child shows the least bit of interest, encourage your child to learn at least one musical instrument. Research has shown that early lessons in music have a strong impact on later development of math skills.

Explain the News. When your child is exposed to news stories and advertisements that provide some pop-statistical analysis or some reporting of graphs or trends, make sure your child understands the concepts they are talking about as well as possible fallacies involved in the report.

If you see a news report of an excessive gain or loss in the Dow Jones Industrial Average, explain what the figure means and why it is important as a gauge of the health of the stock market. During elections, as updates come in, watch the returns with your child and explain why some news services project winners, for example, with only a small percentage of precincts reporting. Pay attention to polls and share pertinent poll results with your children.

Family Calendar. Keep a family calendar in a prominent place to track important family dates such as birthdays, parties, holidays, and so on. Make it a habit to check the calendar each day with your child.

It's about Time! Buy your child his own watch or a clock for his room. There are plenty of interesting, child-friendly clocks on the market that both amuse and teach the finer points of telling time.

Geometry

Parents may think of geometry as an advanced version of mathematics not introduced until high school, but these days children begin learning about shapes as early as kindergarten.

Finding Perimeters

Most schools introduce the concept of perimeters in second grade, usually limited to judging the distance around objects with straight sides. At first, your child will be introduced to simple three- and four-sided objects. By late second grade to early third grade, he will be able to expand this skill to figures that have uneven sides and will become familiar with finding perimeters for figures with more than four sides.

Matching Shapes

The ability to match shapes requires development of nonverbal, symbolic logic skills. By second grade, your child should be quite good at matching simple, familiar shapes he learned during kindergarten and first grade, such as triangles, circles, and rectangles, even when they are different sizes.

Plane and Solid Figures

Kindergartners and first graders learn to identify figures by rote: They see a star and learn to label it "star." They see a drawing of a cube and label it "cube" or "box." By second grade, your child will begin to label figures verbally and be able to name their characteristics. For example, most middle second graders are able to differentiate a square and rectangle by saying, "They both have four sides, but a square's sides are the same length. On a rectangle, the sides opposite each other are the same, but all four sides don't have to be the same." They may even be able to add, "All squares are rectangles, but not all rectangles are squares." They should be able to verbally describe and name the properties of other common shapes, such as triangles, cubes, cones, spheres, stars, and cylinders.

Your second grader may surprise you by noticing: "Your pill box is the shape of a cylinder!" Many children at this age enjoy making a game of identifying shapes in their everyday world, such as pointing out that the weeding tool you use in the garden is triangle-shaped.

Understanding Spatial Relations

Children generally begin to learn elementary spatial relationships, such as over, under, in front of, and behind, during their kindergarten years, but many of them don't develop a firm command of such relationships until second grade. By late second grade, your child should be able to name simple spatial relationships quickly, accurately, and automatically. At the same time, he should be able to extend his grasp of simple spatial relationships to more complex relationships.

Practice Skill: Geometry

Directions: Read the following questions and choose the correct answer.

1 Find the perimeter of this figure.

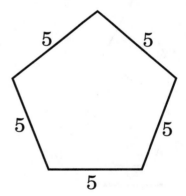

Ⓐ 10

Ⓑ 15

Ⓒ 20

Ⓓ 25

2 Choose the shape that is NOT the same as this one.

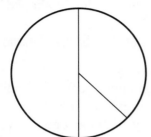

Ⓐ    Ⓑ

Ⓒ   Ⓓ

3 Which shape has the most sides?

Ⓐ

Ⓑ

Ⓒ

Ⓓ

4 Which shape always has four sides of equal length?

Ⓐ square

Ⓑ rectangle

Ⓒ triangle

Ⓓ parallelogram

5 Which animal is <u>farthest away from</u> the food bowl?

Ⓐ puppy   Ⓑ bird

Ⓒ snake   Ⓓ lion

6 Which picture shows a pencil going <u>through</u> the apple?

Ⓐ

Ⓑ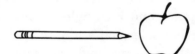

Ⓒ

Ⓓ

7 Which answer below describes this picture?

Ⓐ The dog is beside the girl.

Ⓑ The girl is over the dog.

Ⓒ The dog is behind the girl.

Ⓓ The girl is in front of the dog.

(See page 114 for answer key.)

Measurement

Estimation requires that children have been exposed to enough measurement situations so that they can draw on that prior knowledge to make educated guesses about various quantities. By second grade, your child should be able to make simple estimations of weight, size, and temperature.

Most second graders are unable to provide an accurate estimate of the specific weight of various objects, such as looking at a dog and stating that it probably weights about 16 pounds. But most are able by this age to compare weights and to judge which of several objects is the closest in weight to some other object.

Second graders are also learning about other types of measurement. Many schools introduce temperature measurements at about second grade. Until recently in the United States, most introduced the Fahrenheit scale at this time, saving metric measurements for a later time. Increasingly, however, schools are introducing metric measurements at the same time they introduce English measurements.

Standard and Metric Units

More and more schools are introducing the English and metric systems of measurement at approximately the same time. By the end of second grade, most students have learned that length is measured in feet and yards or in centimeters and meters. However, most won't be able to perform sophisticated conversions, such as from inches to centimeters or from gallons to liters, without referring to a conversion chart.

By the end of second grade, your child should be able to use whatever measuring device is available, such as a yardstick or a meter stick, although many will still be confused regarding which is which.

Practice Skill: Measurement

Directions: Look at the following pictures and answer the questions about each picture.

8 Choose which one weighs about the same as the baby:

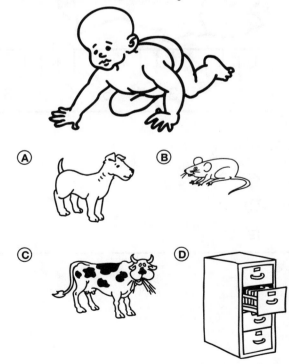

9 About how many feet tall is this notebook?

Ⓐ 2

Ⓑ 4

Ⓒ 1

Ⓓ 5

10 About how many inches long is the fish?

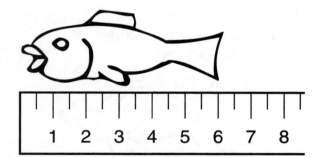

Ⓐ 12

Ⓑ 3

Ⓒ 9

Ⓓ 6

11 Which picture shows something that might happen when the temperature outside is the same as on the thermometer below?

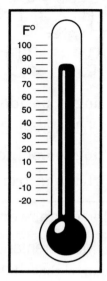

Ⓐ

Ⓑ

Ⓒ

Ⓓ

12 Look at the fishing rod and the fish. Which number tells about how many fish long the fishing rod is?

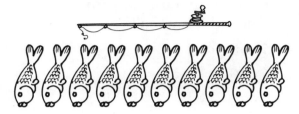

- (A) 10
- (B) 4
- (C) 6
- (D) 5

13 How many horses tall is the tree?

- (A) 1
- (B) 4
- (C) 2
- (D) 5

14 If we want to measure how far the puppy is from the tree, which two ways can we measure the distance?

- (A) feet and liters
- (B) yards and meters
- (C) feet and grams
- (D) meters and liters

15 How long is this piece of string?

1 2 3 4 5 6 7
centimeters

- (A) 7 inches
- (B) 3 centimeters
- (C) 7 centimeters
- (D) 10 inches

(See page 114 for answer key.)

Word Problems

Most second graders are not only much stronger in using basic mathematical operations, but they are also be better able to understand what they hear and read. These abilities, along with more mature reasoning skills, help them do a better job in solving word problems. Because solving word problems requires both the ability to perform the calculations and the logical skills to set up the calculations, word problems are doubly difficult for your child to solve.

What Tests May Ask

You can be sure that standardized tests for the second grade will include at least a few word problems. The tests will present a few simple sentences requiring students to either add or subtract to find the answer. They must then choose the correct answer from a group of possible responses.

Practice Skill: Word Problems

Parents: Read the following problems to your child and have him answer the questions.

16 Caitlin made muffins for the bake sale at school. One muffin pan makes 12 muffins, and the other muffin pan makes 8 muffins. How many muffins would they make altogether?

Ⓐ 18
Ⓑ 24
Ⓒ 16
Ⓓ 20

17 Uncle Jack wanted to make grape juice. He sent Lisa, Jackie, and Billy to pick grapes. He told them to pick four cups of grapes each. How many cups of grapes did Uncle Jack need?

Ⓐ 3
Ⓑ 6
Ⓒ 9
Ⓓ 12

(See page 114 for answer key.)

Time

As your child's brain continues to develop between ages 7 and 9, you will see a big change in his awareness of the world around him: time, place, person, and situation. This ability will continue to develop as he matures. Although your child probably began learning some elementary time concepts at earlier ages, your second grader will learn new time concepts and become more competent and automatic in others.

Reading a Calendar

Many second graders have a very pleasant surprise when they can suddenly understand what calendars are and how we use them, although many early second graders are a bit confused about the order of months and which months have how many days. They can't calculate the number of days between two dates across months, but most are ready to begin to learn such concepts.

Initially, they'll remember there are seven days in a week, although many will be confused why the first day of the week is Sunday, not Monday. With gentle guidance and demonstration, most children are able to construct calendars with seven days in a week, with weeks beginning on Sunday, and with months consisting of 28, 29, 30, or 31 days.

Telling Time

Since the advent of digital clocks on everything from coffee makers to VCRs to clipboards, lunch boxes, and cars, most children learn to tell time on digital clocks during kindergarten or first grade. As technology changes, it's becoming less and less necessary to learn how to set the time on analog watches. In fact, many elementary school teachers have complained that with so many digital watches and clocks in their lives, many children can't tell time on an analog clock until second grade.

Most second graders are already familiar with 60-second minutes, 60-minute hours, and 24-hour days, which they learned about in kindergarten and first grade from reading digital clocks. Certainly it's reasonable to expect them to be able, by middle second grade, to tell time accurately in 5-minute increments on an analog clock. By the end of second grade, they should be able to tell time to the minute on an analog clock.

Practice Skill: Time

Directions: Look at the calendar below and answer the following questions:

May

Sunday	Monday	Tuesday	Wednesday	Thursday	Friday	Saturday
					1	2
3	4	5	6	7	8	9
10	11	12	13	14	15	16
17	18	19	20	21	22	23
24	25	26	27	28	29	30
31						

18 Carlos' class is going to celebrate Cinco de Mayo, which is on May 5. What day of the week will Cinco de Mayo be?

Ⓐ Monday

Ⓑ Tuesday

Ⓒ Thursday

Ⓓ Saturday

19 On May 13, Janey's mother reminded her that she had a dentist appointment next Tuesday. What date of the month is Janey's dentist appointment?

Ⓐ May 13   Ⓑ May 12

Ⓒ May 19   Ⓓ May 15

20 Choose the two clocks that tell the same time.

Ⓐ

Ⓑ

Ⓒ

Ⓓ

(See page 114 for answer key.)

By early to middle second grade, most children can judge elapsed time in whole-hour units not crossing the 12:00 mark on both digital and analog clocks. As their ability to tell time increases, along with more accurate and automatic understanding of 60-second minutes and 60-minute hours, their ability to judge elapsed time down to the minute will increase. They are already familiar with elapsed time from learning the school schedule (for example, that music, gym, and art classes last for 50 minutes). As their command of telling time increases, usually by the end of second grade, most children are able to tell elapsed time in hours and minutes.

21 Joshua started his test at 9:15 a.m. His teacher said that he had exactly 50 minutes to finish the test. When must he be finished with his test?

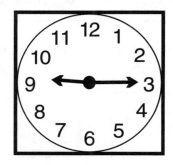

Ⓐ 10:05 a.m.

Ⓑ 10:15 a.m.

Ⓒ 11:00 a.m.

Ⓓ 11:05 a.m.

22 Angie likes to get a good night's sleep. She went to bed at 9:00 p.m. and slept until 7 a.m. How many hours did she sleep?

Ⓐ 8

Ⓑ 9

Ⓒ 11

Ⓓ 10

23 Jamie's physical education teacher said that she was going to use a stopwatch to time how long it took each child to run from home plate to first base on the softball field. When she writes down each child's time, what units of time will she write down?

Ⓐ hours

Ⓑ minutes

Ⓒ seconds

Ⓓ days

24 Jeff and his grandfather baked chocolate oatmeal muffins. They put them in the oven and set the timer. What units of time would Jeff and his grandfather use to time the muffins?

Ⓐ hours

Ⓑ seconds

Ⓒ minutes

Ⓓ days

(See page 114 for answer key.)

Money

Many children have only a very vague sense of money up until the beginning of second grade; but by the end of second grade your child should have a basic understanding of coins and their values. Second graders should be able to automatically calculate the values of each coin and to make change.

What Tests May Ask

Understanding coins is certainly a component of standardized testing. Standardized tests ask a variety of questions about money, including how many of a certain coin are needed to add up to a certain amount. Some tests provide pictures of coins and ask children to choose which grouping of coins equals a certain amount.

Practice Skill: Money

Directions: Read the following questions and choose the correct answer.

25 How many dimes does it take to equal the value of two quarters?

Ⓐ 5   Ⓑ 2

Ⓒ 3   Ⓓ 10

26 Kristie bought a Zagnut for 52 cents. The cashier added 3 cents tax to the price. Which combination of coins would Kristie need to pay the exact cost of the candy?

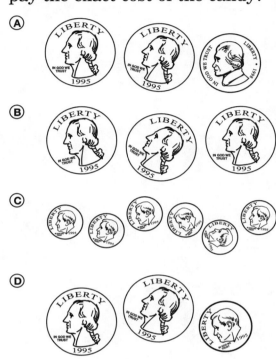

(See page 114 for answer key.)

Web Sites and Resources for More Information

Homework

Homework Central
http://www.HomeworkCentral.com
Terrific site for students, parents, and teachers, filled with information, projects, and more.

Win the Homework Wars
(Sylvan Learning Centers)
http://www.educate.com/online/qa_peters.html

Reading and Grammar Help

Born to Read: How to Raise a Reader
http://www.ala.org/alsc/raise_a_reader.html

Guide to Grammar and Writing
http://webster.commnet.edu/hp/pages/darling/grammar.htm
Help with "plague words and phrases," grammar FAQs, sentence parts, punctuation, rules for common usage.

Internet Public Library: Reading Zone
http://www.ipl.org/cgi-bin/youth/youth.out

Keeping Kids Reading and Writing
http://www.tiac.net/users/maryl/

U.S. Dept. of Education: Helping Your Child Learn to Read
http://www.ed.gov/pubs/parents/Reading/index.html

Math Help

Center for Advancement of Learning
http://www.muskingum.edu/%7Ecal/database/Math2.html
Substitution and memory strategies for math.

Center for Advancement of Learning
http://www.muskingum.edu/%7Ecal/database/Math1.html
General tips and suggestions.

Math.com
http://www.math.com
The world of math online.

Math.com
http://www.math.com/student/testprep.html
Get ready for standardized tests.

Math.com: Homework Help in Math
http://www.math.com/students/homework.html

Math.com: Math for Homeschoolers
http://www.math.com/parents/homeschool.html

The Math Forum: Problems and Puzzles
http://forum.swarthmore.edu/library/resource_types/problems_puzzles
Lots of fun math puzzles and problems for grades K through 12.

The Math Forum: Math Tips and Tricks
http://forum.swarthmore.edu/k12/mathtips/mathtips.html

Tips on Testing

Books on Test Preparation
http://www.testbooksonline.com/preHS.asp
This site provides printed resources for parents who wish to help their children prepare for standardized school tests.

Core Knowledge Web Site
http://www.coreknowledge.org/
Site dedicated to providing resources for parents; based on the books of E. D. Hirsch, Jr., who wrote the *What Your X Grader Needs to Know* series.

Family Education Network
http://www.familyeducation.com/article/0,1120,
1-6219,00.html
This report presents some of the arguments against current standardized testing practices in the public schools. The site also provides links to family activities that help kids learn.

Math.com
http://www.math.com/students/testprep.html
Get ready for standardized tests.

Standardized Tests
http://arc.missouri.edu/k12/
K through 12 assessment tools and know-how.

Parents: Testing in Schools

KidSource: Talking to Your Child's Teacher about Standardized Tests
http://www.kidsource.com/kidsource/content2/
talking.assessment.k12.4.html
This site provides basic information to help parents understand their children's test results and provides pointers for how to discuss the results with their children's teachers.

eSCORE.com: State Test and Education Standards
http://www.eSCORE.com
Find out if your child meets the necessary requirements for your local schools. A Web site with experts from Brazelton Institute and Harvard's Project Zero.

Overview of States' Assessment Programs
http://ericae.net/faqs/

Parent Soup
Education Central: Standardized Tests
http://www.parentsoup.com/edcentral/testing
A parent's guide to standardized testing in the schools, written from a parent advocacy standpoint.

National Center for Fair and Open Testing, Inc. (FairTest)
342 Broadway
Cambridge, MA 02139
(617) 864-4810
http://www.fairtest.org

National Parent Information Network
http://npin.org

Publications for Parents from the U.S. Department of Education
http://www.ed.gov/pubs/parents/
An ever-changing list of information for parents available from the U.S. Department of Education.

State of the States Report
http://www.edweek.org/sreports/qc99/states/
indicators/in-intro.htm
A report on testing and achievement in the 50 states.

Testing: General Information

Academic Center for Excellence
http://www.acekids.com

American Association for Higher Education Assessment
http://www.aahe.org/assessment/web.htm

American Educational Research Association (AERA)
http://aera.net
An excellent link to reports on American education, including reports on the controversy over standardized testing.

American Federation of Teachers
555 New Jersey Avenue, NW
Washington, D.C. 20011

Association of Test Publishers Member Products and Services

http://www.testpublishers.org/memserv.htm

Education Week on the Web

http://www.edweek.org

ERIC Clearinghouse on Assessment and Evaluation

1131 Shriver Lab
University of Maryland
College Park, MD 20742
http://ericae.net

A clearinghouse of information on assessment and education reform.

FairTest: The National Center for Fair and Open Testing

http://fairtest.org/facts/ntfact.htm
http://fairtest.org/

The National Center for Fair and Open Testing is an advocacy organization working to end the abuses, misuses, and flaws of standardized testing and to ensure that evaluation of students and workers is fair, open, and educationally sound. This site provides many links to fact sheets, opinion papers, and other sources of information about testing.

National Congress of Parents and Teachers

700 North Rush Street
Chicago, Illinois 60611

National Education Association

1201 16th Street, NW
Washington, DC 20036

National School Boards Association

http://www.nsba.org

A good source for information on all aspects of public education, including standardized testing.

Testing Our Children: A Report Card on State Assessment Systems

http://www.fairtest.org/states/survey.htm

Report of testing practices of the states, with graphical links to the states and a critique of fair testing practices in each state.

Trends in Statewide Student Assessment Programs: A Graphical Summary

http://www.ccsso.org/survey96.html

Results of annual survey of states' departments of public instruction regarding their testing practices.

U.S. Department of Education

http://www.ed.gov/

Web Links for Parents Who Want to Help Their Children Achieve

http://www.liveandlearn.com/learn.html

This page offers many Web links to free and for-sale information and materials for parents who want to help their children do well in school. Titles include such free offerings as the Online Colors Game and questionnaires to determine whether your child is ready for school.

What Should Parents Know about Standardized Testing in the Schools?

http://www.rusd.k12.ca.us/parents/standard.html

An online brochure about standardized testing in the schools, with advice regarding how to become an effective advocate for your child.

Test Publishers Online

ACT: Information for Life's Transitions

http://www.act.org

American Guidance Service, Inc.

http://www.agsnet.com

Ballard & Tighe Publishers

http://www.ballard-tighe.com

Consulting Psychologists Press

http://www.cpp-db.com

CTB McGraw-Hill

http://www.ctb.com

Educational Records Bureau

http://www.erbtest.org/index.html

Educational Testing Service

http://www.ets.org

General Educational Development (GED) Testing Service
http://www.acenet.edu/calec/ged/home.html

Harcourt Brace Educational Measurement
http://www.hbem.com

Piney Mountain Press—A Cyber-Center for Career and Applied Learning
http://www.pineymountain.com

ProEd Publishing
http://www.proedinc.com

Riverside Publishing Company
http://www.hmco.com/hmco/riverside

Stoelting Co.
http://www.stoeltingco.com

Sylvan Learning Systems, Inc.
http://www.educate.com

Touchstone Applied Science Associates, Inc. (TASA)
http://www.tasa.com

Tests Online

(*Note:* We don't endorse tests; some may not have technical documentation. Evaluate the quality of any testing program before making decisions based on its use.)

Edutest, Inc.
http://www.edutest.com
Edutest is an Internet-accessible testing service that offers criterion-referenced tests for elementary school students, based upon the standards for K through 12 learning and achievement in the states of Virginia, California, and Florida.

Virtual Knowledge
http://www.smarterkids.com
This commercial service, which enjoys a formal partnership with Sylvan Learning Centers, offers a line of skills assessments for preschool through grade 9 for use in the classroom or the home. For free online sample tests, see the Virtual Test Center.

Read More about It

Abbamont, Gary W. *Test Smart: Ready-to-Use Test-Taking Strategies and Activities for Grades 5–12. Upper Saddle River,* NJ: Prentice Hall Direct, 1997.

Cookson, Peter W., and Joshua Halberstam. *A Parent's Guide to Standardized Tests in School: How to Improve Your Child's Chances for Success.* New York: Learning Express, 1998.

Frank, Steven, and Stephen Frank. *Test-Taking Secrets: Study Better, Test Smarter, and Get Great Grades (The Backpack Study Series).* Holbrook, MA: Adams Media Corporation, 1998.

Gilbert, Sara Dulaney. *How to Do Your Best on Tests: A Survival Guide.* New York: Beech Tree Books, 1998.

Gruber, Gary. *Dr. Gary Gruber's Essential Guide to Test-Taking for Kids, Grades 3–5.* New York: William Morrow & Co., 1986.

——. *Gary Gruber's Essential Guide to Test-Taking for Kids, Grades 6, 7, 8, 9.* New York: William Morrow & Co., 1997.

Leonhardt, Mary. *99 Ways to Get Kids to Love Reading and 100 Books They'll Love.* New York: Crown, 1997.

——. *Parents Who Love Reading, Kids Who Don't: How It Happens and What You Can Do about It.* New York: Crown, 1995.

McGrath, Barbara B. *The Baseball Counting Book.* Watertown, MA: Charlesbridge, 1999.

——. *More M&M's Brand Chocolate Candies Math.* Watertown, MA: Charlesbridge, 1998.

Mokros, Janice R. *Beyond Facts & Flashcards: Exploring Math with Your Kids.* Portsmouth, NH: Heinemann, 1996.

Romain, Trevor, and Elizabeth Verdick. *True or False?: Tests Stink!* Minneapolis: Free Spirit Publishing Co., 1999.

Schartz, Eugene M. *How to Double Your Child's Grades in School: Build Brilliance and Leadership into Your Child—from Kindergarten to College—in Just 5 Minutes a Day.* New York: Barnes & Noble, 1999.

Taylor, Kathe, and Sherry Walton. *Children at the Center: A Workshop Approach to Standardized Test Preparation, K–8.* Portsmouth, NH: Heinemann, 1998.

Tobia, Sheila. *Overcoming Math Anxiety.* New York: W. W. Norton & Company, Inc., 1995.

Tufariello, Ann Hunt. *Up Your Grades: Proven Strategies for Academic Success.* Lincolnwood, IL: VGM Career Horizons, 1996.

Vorderman, Carol. *How Math Works.* Pleasantville, NY: Reader's Digest Association, Inc., 1996.

Zahler, Kathy A. *50 Simple Things You Can Do to Raise a Child Who Loves to Read.* New York: IDG Books, 1997.

What Your Child's Test Scores Mean

Several weeks or months after your child has taken standardized tests, you will receive a report such as the TerraNova Home Report found in Figures 1 and 2. You will receive similar reports if your child has taken other tests. We briefly examine what information the reports include.

Look at the first page of the Home Report. Note that the chart provides labeled bars showing the child's performance. Each bar is labeled with the child's National Percentile for that skill area. When you know how to interpret them, national percentiles can be the most useful scores you encounter on reports such as this. Even when you are confronted with different tests that use different scale scores, you can always interpret percentiles the same way, regardless of the test. A percentile tells the percent of students who score at or below that level. A percentile of 25, for example, means that 25 percent of children taking the test scored at or below that score. (It also means that 75 percent of students scored above that score.) Note that the average is always at the 50th percentile.

On the right side of the graph on the first page of the report, the publisher has designated the ranges of scores that constitute average, above average, and below average. You can also use this slightly more precise key for interpreting percentiles:

PERCENTILE RANGE	LEVEL
2 and Below	Deficient
3–8	Borderline
9–23	Low Average
24–75	Average
76–97	High Average
98 and Up	Superior

The second page of the Home report provides a listing of the child's strengths and weaknesses, along with keys for mastery, partial mastery, and non-mastery of the skills. Scoring services determine these breakdowns based on the child's scores as compared with those from the national norm group.

Your child's teacher or guidance counselor will probably also receive a profile report similar to the TerraNova Individual Profile Report, shown in Figures 3 and 4. That report will be kept in your child's permanent record. The first aspect of this report to notice is that the scores are expressed both numerically and graphically.

First look at the score bands under National Percentile. Note that the scores are expressed as bands, with the actual score represented by a dot within each band. The reason we express the scores as bands is to provide an idea of the amount by which typical scores may vary for each student. That is, each band represents a

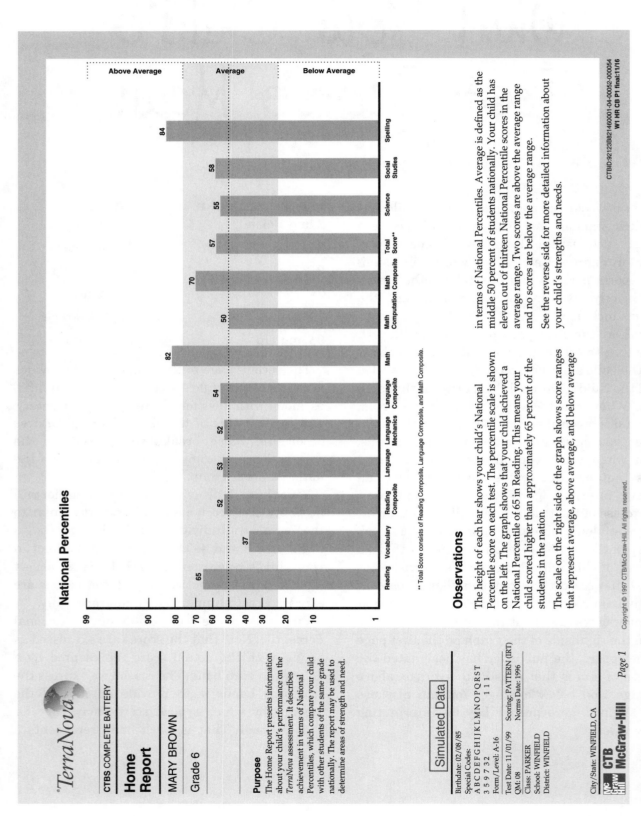

Figure 1 (SOURCE: CTB/McGraw-Hill, copyright © 1997. All rights reserved. Reproduced with permission.)

TerraNova

CTBS COMPLETE BATTERY

Home Report

MARY BROWN

Grade 6

Purpose

This page of the Home Report presents information about your child's strengths and needs. This information is provided to help you monitor your child's academic growth.

Simulated Data

Birthdate: 02/08/85
Special Codes:
A B C D E F G H I J K L M N O P Q R S T
3 5 9 7 3 2   1 1 1
Form/Level: A-16   Scoring: PATTERN (IRT)
QM: 08   Norms Date: 1996

Test Date: 11/01/99

Class: PARKER
School: WINFIELD
District: WINFIELD

City/State: WINFIELD, CA

CTB / McGraw-Hill   *Page 2*

Strengths

Reading
- Basic Understanding
- Analyze Text

Vocabulary
- Word Meaning
- Words in Context

Language
- Editing Skills
- Sentence Structure

Language Mechanics
- Sentences, Phrases, Clauses

Mathematics
- Computation and Numerical Estimation
- Operation Concepts

Mathematics Computation
- Add Whole Numbers
- Multiply Whole Numbers

Science
- Life Science
- Inquiry Skills

Social Studies
- Geographic Perspectives
- Economic Perspectives

Spelling
- Vowels
- Consonants

Key ● **Mastery**

Needs

Reading
- ◑ Evaluate and Extend Meaning
- ○ Identify Reading Strategies

Vocabulary
- ○ Multimeaning Words

Language
- ◑ Writing Strategies

Language Mechanics
- ○ Writing Conventions

Mathematics
- ◑ Measurement
- ◑ Geometry and Spatial Sense

Mathematics Computation
- ○ Percents

Science
- ○ Earth and Space Science

Social Studies
- ◑ Historical and Cultural Perspectives

Spelling
No area of needs were identified for this content area

Key ◑ **Partial Mastery**   ○ **Non-Mastery**

General Interpretation

The left column shows your child's best areas of performance. In each case, your child has reached mastery level. The column at the right shows the areas within each test section where your child's scores are the lowest. In these cases, your child has not reached mastery level, although he or she may have reached partial mastery.

Figure 2   (SOURCE: CTB/McGraw-Hill, copyright © 1997. All rights reserved. Reproduced with permission.)

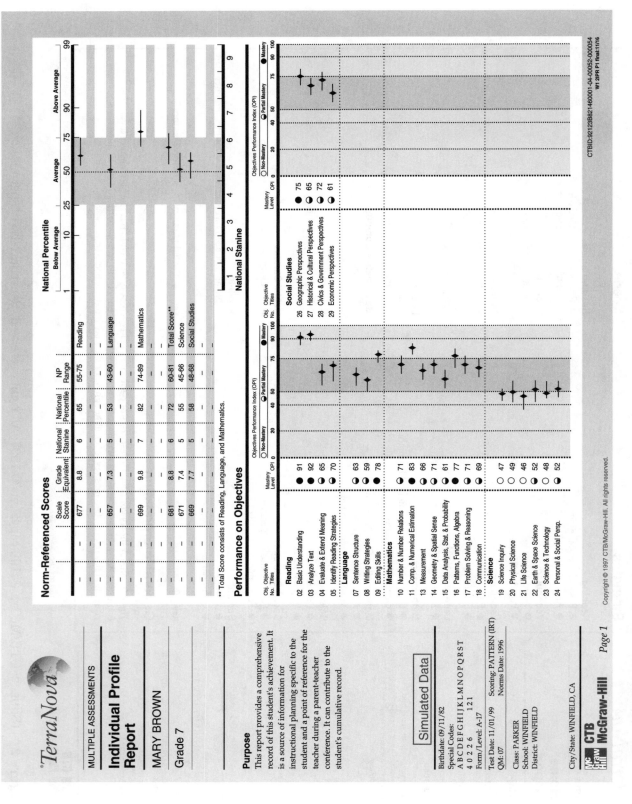

Figure 3 (Source: CTB/McGraw-Hill, copyright © 1997. All rights reserved. Reproduced with permission.)

Observations

Norm-Referenced Scores

The top section of the report presents information about this student's achievement in several different ways. The National Percentile (NP) data and graph indicate how this student performed compared to students of the same grade nationally. The National Percentile range indicates that if this student had taken the test numerous times the scores would have fallen within the range shown. The shaded area on the graph represents the average range of scores, usually defined as the middle 50 percent of students nationally. Scores in the area to the right of the shading are above the average range. Scores in the area to the left of the shading are below the average range.

In Reading, for example, this student achieved a National Percentile rank of 65. This student scored higher than 65 percent of the students nationally. This score is in the average range. This student has a total of five scores in the average range. One score is in the above average range. No scores are in the below average range.

Performance on Objectives

The next section of the report presents performance on the objectives. Each objective is measured by a minimum of 4 items. The Objectives Performance Index (OPI) provides an estimate of the number of items that a student could be expected to answer correctly if there had been 100 items for that objective. The OPI is used to indicate mastery of each objective. An OPI of 75 and above characterizes Mastery. An OPI between 50 and 74 indicates Partial Mastery, and an OPI below 50 indicates Non-Mastery. The two-digit number preceding the objective title identifies the objective, which is fully described in the Teacher's Guide to *TerraNova*. The bands on either side of the diamonds indicate the range within which the student's test scores would fall if the student were tested numerous times.

In Reading, for example, this student could be expected to respond correctly to 91 out of 100 items measuring Basic Understanding. If this student had taken the test numerous times the OPI for this objective would have fallen between 82 and 93.

Teacher Notes

_____

_____

_____

_____

_____

_____

MULTIPLE ASSESSMENTS

Individual Profile Report

MARY BROWN

Grade 7

Purpose

The Observations section of the Individual Profile Report gives teachers and parents information to interpret this report. This page is a narrative description of the data on the other side.

Simulated Data

Birthdate: 09/11/82
Special Codes:
A B C D E F G H I J K L M N O P Q R S T
4 0 2 2 6   1 2 1
Form/Level: A-17

Test Date: 11/01/99   Scoring: PATTERN (IRT)
QM: 08   Norms Date: 1996

Class: PARKER
School: WINFIELD
District: WINFIELD

City/State: WINFIELD, CA

Page 2

Figure 4 (SOURCE: CTB/McGraw-Hill, copyright © 1997. All rights reserved. Reproduced with permission.)

TerraNova

MULTIPLE ASSESSMENTS

Student Performance Level Report

KEN ALLEN

Grade 4

Purpose
This report describes this student's achievement in terms of five performance levels for each content area. The meaning of these levels is described on the back of this page. Performance levels are a new way of describing achievement.

Simulated Data

Birthdate: 02/08/86
Special Codes:
A B C D E F G H I J K L M N O P Q R S T
3 5 9 7 3 2   1 1 1
Form/Level: A-14
Test Date: 04/15/97   Scoring: PATTERN (IRT)
QM: 31   Norms Date: 1996

Class: SCHWARZ
School: WINFIELD
District: GREEN VALLEY

City/State: WINFIELD, CA

Performance Levels	Reading	Language	Mathematics	Science	Social Studies
5 Advanced					
4 Proficient					
3 Nearing Proficiency	✓				✓
2 Progressing	✓	✓	✓	✓	✓
1 Step 1	✓	✓	✓	✓	✓

Partially Proficient (covers levels 3, 2, 1)

Observations

Performance level scores provide a measure of what students *can do* in terms of the content and skills assessed by *TerraNova*, and typically found in curricula for Grades 3, 4, and 5. It is desirable to work towards achieving a Level 4 (Proficient) or Level 5 (Advanced) by the end of Grade 5.

The number of check marks indicates the performance level this student reached in each content area. For example, this student reached Level 3 in Reading and Social Studies.

The performance level indicates this student can perform the majority of what is described for that level and even more of what is described for the levels below. The student may also be capable of performing some of the things described in the next higher level, but not enough to have reached that level of performance.

For example, this student can perform the majority of what is described for Level 3 in Reading and even more of what is described for Level 2 and Level 1 in Reading. This student may also be capable of performing some of what is described for Level 4 in Reading.

For each content area look at the skills and knowledge described in the next higher level. These are the competencies this student needs to demonstrate to show academic growth.

Figure 5 (SOURCE: CTB/McGraw-Hill, copyright © 1997. All rights reserved. Reproduced with permission.)

Performance Levels (Grades 3, 4, 5)	Reading	Language	Mathematics	Science	Social Studies
5 Advanced	Students use analogies to generalize. They identify a paraphrase of concepts or ideas in texts. They can indicate thought processes that led them to a previous answer. In written responses, they demonstrate understanding of an implied theme, assess intent of passage information, and provide justification as well as support for their answers.	Students understand logical development in paragraph structure. They identify essential information from notes. They recognize the effect of prepositional phrases on subject-verb agreement. They find and correct at least 4 out of 6 errors when editing simple narratives. They correct run-on and incomplete sentences in more complex texts. They can eliminate all errors when editing their own work.	Students locate decimals on a number line; compute with decimals and fractions; read scale drawings; find areas; identify geometric transformations; construct and label bar graphs; find simple probabilities; find averages; use patterns in data to solve problems; use multiple strategies and concepts to solve unfamiliar problems; express mathematical ideas and explain the problem-solving process.	Students understand a broad range of grade level scientific concepts, such as the structure of Earth and instinctive behavior. They know terminology, such as decomposers, fossil fuel, eclipse, and buoyancy. Knowledge of more complex environmental issues includes, for example, the positive consequences of a forest fire. Students can process and interpret more detailed tables and graphs. They can suggest improvements to experimental design, such as running more trials.	Students consistently demonstrate skills such as synthesizing information from two sources (e.g., a document and a map). They show understanding of the democratic process and global environmental issues, and know the location of continents and major countries. They analyze and summarize information from multiple sources in early American history. They thoroughly explain both sides of an issue and give complete and detailed written answers to questions.
4 Proficient	Students interpret figures of speech. They recognize paraphrase of text information and retrieve information to complete forms. In more complex texts, they identify themes, main ideas, or author purpose/point of view. They analyze and apply information in graphic and text form, make reasonable generalizations, and draw conclusions. In written responses, they can identify key elements from text.	Students select the best supporting sentences for a topic sentence. They use compound predicates to combine sentences. They identify simple subjects and predicates, recognize correct usage when confronted with two types of errors, and find and correct at least 3 out of 6 errors when editing simple narratives. They can edit their own work with only minor errors.	Students compare, order, and round whole numbers; know place value to thousands; identify fractions; use computation and estimation strategies; relate multiplication to addition; measure to nearest half-inch and centimeter; measure and find perimeters; estimate measures; find elapsed times; combine and subdivide shapes; identify parallel lines; interpret tables and graphs; solve two-step problems.	Students have a range of specific science knowledge, including details about animal adaptations and classification, states of matter, and the geology of Earth. They recognize scientific words such as habitat, gravity, and mass. They understand the usefulness of computers. They understand reasons for conserving natural resources. Understanding of experimentation includes analyzing purpose, interpreting data, and selecting tools to gather data.	Students demonstrate skills such as making inferences, using historical documents and analyzing maps to determine the economic strengths of a region. They understand the function of currency in various cultures and supply and demand. They summarize information from multiple sources, recognize relationships, determine relevance of information, and show global awareness. They propose solutions to real-world problems and support ideas with appropriate details.
3 Nearing Proficiency	Students use context clues and structural analysis to determine word meaning. They recognize homonyms and antonyms in grade-level text. They identify important details, sequence, cause and effect, and lessons embedded in the text. They interpret characters' feelings and apply information to new situations. In written responses, they can express an opinion and support it.	Students identify irrelevant sentences in paragraphs and select the best place to insert new information. They recognize faulty sentence construction. They can combine simple sentences with conjunctions and use simple subordination of phrases/clauses. They identify reference sources. They recognize correct conventions for dates, closings, and place names in informal correspondence.	Students identify even and odd numbers; subtract whole numbers with regrouping; multiply and divide by one-digit numbers; identify simple fractions; measure with ruler to nearest inch; tell time to nearest fifteen minutes; recognize and classify common shapes; recognize symmetry; subdivide shapes; complete bar graphs; extend numerical and geometric patterns; apply simple logical reasoning.	Students are familiar with the life cycles of plants and animals. They can identify an example of a cold-blooded animal. They infer what once existed from fossil evidence. They understand the water cycle. They know science and society issues such as recycling and sources of pollution. They can sequence technological advances. They extrapolate data, devise a simple classification scheme, and determine the purpose of a simple experiment.	Students demonstrate skills in organizing information. They use time lines, product and global maps, and cardinal directions. They understand simple cause and effect relationships and historical documents. They recognize simple geographical terms and sequence events, associate holidays with events, and classify natural resources. They compare life in different times and understand some economic concepts related to products, jobs, and the environment. They give some detail in written responses.
2 Progressing	Students identify synonyms for grade-level words, and use context clues to define common words. They make simple inferences and predictions based on text. They identify characters' feelings. They can transfer information from text to graphic form, or from graphic form to text. In written responses, they can provide limited support for their answers.	Students identify the use of correct verb tenses and correct use of pronouns. They complete paragraphs by selecting an appropriate topic sentence. They select correct adjective forms.	Students know ordinal numbers; solve coin combination problems; count by tens; add whole numbers with regrouping; have basic estimation skills; understand addition property of zero; write and identify number sentences describing simple situations; read calendars; identify appropriate measurement tools; recognize congruent figures; use simple coordinate grids; read common tables and graphs.	Students recognize that plants decompose and become part of soil. They can classify a plant as a vegetable. They recognize that camouflage relates to survival. They recognize simple science terms such as hibernate. They have an understanding of human impact on the environment and are familiar with causes of pollution. They find the correct bar graph to represent given data and transfer data appropriate for middle elementary grades to a bar graph.	Students demonstrate simple information-processing skills such as using basic maps and keys. They recognize simple geographical terms, types of jobs, modes of transportation, and natural resources. They connect a human need with an appropriate community service. They identify some early famous presidents and know the capital of the United States. Their written answers are partially complete.
1 Step 1	Students select pictured representations of ideas and identify stated details contained in simple texts. In written responses, they can select and transfer information from charts.	Students supply subjects to complete sentences. They identify the correct use of pronouns. They edit for the correct use of end marks and initial capital letters, and identify the correct convention for greetings in letters.	Students read and recognize numbers to 1000; identify real-world use of two-digit numbers; add and subtract two-digit numbers without regrouping; identify addition situations; recognize and complete simple geometric and numerical patterns.	Students recognize basic adaptations for living in the water, identify an animal that is hatched from an egg, and associate an organism with its correct environment. They identify an object as metal. They have some understanding of conditions on the moon. They supply one way a computer can be useful. They associate an instrument like a telescope with a field of study.	Students are developing fundamental social studies skills such as locating and classifying basic information. They locate information in pictures and read and complete simple bar graphs related to social studies concepts and contexts. They can connect some city buildings with their functions and recognize certain historical objects.

Partially Proficient (levels 2 and 1)

W1 SPLR P2:11/02

IMPORTANT: Each performance level, depicted on the other side, indicates the student can perform the majority of what is described for that level and even more of what is described for the levels below. The student may also be capable of performing some of the things described in the next higher level, but not enough to have reached that level.

Figure 6 (SOURCE: CTB/McGraw-Hill, copyright © 1997. All rights reserved. Reproduced with permission.)

confidence interval. In these reports, we usually report either a 90 percent or 95 percent confidence interval. Interpret a confidence interval this way: Suppose we report a 90 percent confidence interval of 25 to 37. This means we estimate that, if the child took the test multiple times, we would expect that child's score to be in the 25 to 37 range 90 percent of the time.

Now look under the section titled Norm-Referenced Scores on the first page of the Individual Profile Report (Figure 3). The farthest column on the right provides the NP Range, which is the National Percentile scores represented by the score bands in the chart.

Next notice the column labeled Grade Equivalent. Theoretically, grade level equivalents equate a student's score in a skill area with the average grade placement of children who made the same score. Many psychologists and test developers would prefer that we stopped reporting grade equivalents, because they can be grossly misleading. For example, the average reading grade level of high school seniors as reported by one of the more popular tests is the eighth grade level. Does that mean that the nation's high school seniors cannot read? No. The way the test publisher calculated grade equivalents was to determine the average test scores for students in grades 4 to 6 and then simply extend the resulting prediction formula to grades 7 to 12. The result is that parents of average high school seniors who take the test in question would mistakenly believe that their seniors are reading four grade levels behind! Stick to the percentile in interpreting your child's scores.

Now look at the columns labeled Scale Score and National Stanine. These are two of a group of scores we also call *standard scores.* In reports for other tests, you may see other standard scores reported, such as Normal Curve Equivalents (NCEs), Z-Scores, and T-Scores. The IQ that we report on intelligence tests, for

example, is a standard score. Standard scores are simply a way of expressing a student's scores in terms of the statistical properties of the scores from the norm group against which we are comparing the child. Although most psychologists prefer to speak in terms of standard scores among themselves, parents are advised to stick to percentiles in interpreting your child's performance.

Now look at the section of the report labeled Performance on Objectives. In this section, the test publisher reports how your child did on the various skills that make up each skills area. Note that the scores on each objective are expressed as a percentile band, and you are again told whether your child's score constitutes mastery, non-mastery, or partial mastery. Note that these scores are made up of tallies of sometimes small numbers of test items taken from sections such as Reading or Math. Because they are calculated from a much smaller number of scores than the main scales are (for example, Sentence Comprehension is made up of fewer items than overall Reading), their scores are less reliable than those of the main scales.

Now look at the second page of the Individual Profile Report (Figure 4). Here the test publisher provides a narrative summary of how the child did on the test. These summaries are computer-generated according to rules provided by the publisher. Note that the results descriptions are more general than those on the previous three report pages. But they allow the teacher to form a general picture of which students are performing at what general skill levels.

Finally, your child's guidance counselor may receive a summary report such as the TerraNova Student Performance Level Report. (See Figures 5 and 6.) In this report, the publisher explains to school personnel what skills the test assessed and generally how proficiently the child tested under each skill.

Which States Require Which Tests

Tables 1 through 3 summarize standardized testing practices in the 50 states and the District of Columbia. This information is constantly changing; the information presented here was accurate as of the date of printing of this book. Many states have changed their testing practices in response to revised accountability legislation, while others have changed the tests they use.

Table 1   State Web Sites: Education and Testing

STATE	GENERAL WEB SITE	STATE TESTING WEB SITE
Alabama	http://www.alsde.edu/	http://www.fairtest.org/states/al.htm
Alaska	www.educ.state.ak.us/	http://www.eed.state.ak.us/tls/Performance Standards/
Arizona	http://www.ade.state.az.us/	http://www.ade.state.az.us/standards/
Arkansas	http://arkedu.k12.ar.us/	http://www.fairtest.org/states/ar.htm
California	http://goldmine.cde.ca.gov/	http://ww.cde.ca.gov/cilbranch/sca/
Colorado	http://www.cde.state.co.us/index_home.htm	http://www.cde.state.co.us/index_assess.htm
Connecticut	http://www.state.ct.us/sde	http://www.state.ct.us/sde/cmt/index.htm
Delaware	http://www.doe.state.de.us/	http://www.doe.state.de.us/aab/index.htm
District of Columbia	http://www.k12.dc.us/dcps/home.html	http://www.k12.dc.us/dcps/data/data_frame2.html
Florida	http://www.firn.edu/doe/	http://www.firn.edu/doe/sas/sasshome.htm
Georgia	http://www.doe.k12.ga.us/	http://www.doe.k12.ga.us/sla/ret/recotest.html
Hawaii	http://kalama.doe.hawaii.edu/upena/	http://www.fairtest.org/states/hi.htm
Idaho	http://www.sde.state.id.us/Dept/	http://www.sde.state.id.us/instruct/ schoolaccount/statetesting.htm
Illinois	http://www.isbe.state.il.us/	http://www.isbe.state.il.us/isat/
Indiana	http://doe.state.in.us/	http://doe.state.in.us/assessment/welcome.html
Iowa	http://www.state.ia.us/educate/index.html	(Tests Chosen Locally)
Kansas	http://www.ksbe.state.ks.us/	http://www.ksbe.state.ks.us/assessment/
Kentucky	http://www.kde.state.ky.us/	http://www.kde.state.ky.us/oaa/
Louisiana	http://www.doe.state.la.us/DOE/asps/home.asp	http://www.doe.state.la.us/DOE/asps/home.asp?I=HISTAKES
Maine	http://janus.state.me.us/education/homepage.htm	http://janus.state.me.us/education/mea/meacompass.htm
Maryland	http://www.msde.state.md.us/	http://www.fairtest.org/states/md.htm
Massachusetts	http://www.doe.mass.edu/	http://www.doe.mass.edu/mcas/
Michigan	http://www.mde.state.mi.us/	http://www.mde.state.mi.us/off/meap/

STATE	GENERAL WEB SITE	STATE TESTING WEB SITE
Minnesota	http://www.educ.state.mn.us/	http://fairtest.org/states/mn.htm
Mississippi	http://mdek12.state.ms.us/	http://fairtest.org/states/ms.htm
Missouri	http://services.dese.state.mo.us/	http://fairtest.org/states/mo.htm
Montana	http://www.metnet.mt.gov/	http://fairtest.org/states/mt.htm
Nebraska	http://nde4.nde.state.ne.us/	http://www.edneb.org/IPS/AppAccrd/ ApprAccrd.html
Nevada	http://www.nsn.k12.nv.us/nvdoe/	http://www.nsn.k12.nv.us/nvdoe/reports/ TerraNova.doc
New Hampshire	http://www.state.nh.us/doe/	http://www.state.nh.us/doe/Assessment/ assessme(NHEIAP).htm
New Jersey	http://ww.state.nj.us/education/	http://www.state.nj.us/njded/stass/index.html
New Mexico	http://sde.state.nm.us/	http://sde.state.nm.us/press/august30a.html
New York	http://www.nysed.gov/	http://www.emsc.nysed.gov/ciai/assess.html
North Carolina	http://www.dpi.state.nc.us/	http://www.dpi.state.nc.us/accountability/ reporting/index.html
North Dakota	http://www.dpi.state.nd.us/dpi/index.htm	http://www.dpi.state.nd.us/dpi/reports/ assess/assess.htm
Ohio	http://www.ode.state.oh.us/	http://www.ode.state.oh.us/ca/
Oklahoma	http://sde.state.ok.us/	http://sde.state.ok.us/acrob/testpack.pdf
Oregon	http://www.ode.state.or.us//	http://www.ode.state.or.us/assmt/index.htm
Pennsylvania	http://www.pde.psu.edu/ http://instruct.ride.ri.net/ride_home_page.html	http://www.fairtest.org/states/pa.htm
Rhode Island		
South Carolina	http://www.state.sc.us/sde/	http://www.state.sc.us/sde/reports/terranov.htm
South Dakota	http://www.state.sd.us/state/executive/deca/	http://www.state.sd.us/state/executive/deca/TA/ McRelReport/McRelReports.htm
Tennessee	http://www.state.tn.us/education/	http://www.state.tn.us/education/tsintro.htm
Texas	http://www.tea.state.tx.us/	http://www.tea.state.tx.us/student.assessment/
Utah	http://www.usoe.k12.ut.us/	http://www.usoe.k12.ut.us/eval.usoeeval.htm
Vermont	http://www.cit.state.vt.us/educ/	http://www.fairtest.org/states/vt.htm

STATE	GENERAL WEB SITE	STATE TESTING WEB SITE
Virginia	http://www.pen.k12.va.us/Anthology/VDOE/	http://www.pen.k12.va.us/VDOE/Assessment/home.shtml
Washington	http://www.k12.wa.us/	http://assessment.ospi.wednet.edu/
West Virginia	http://wvde.state.wv.us/	http://www.fairtest.org/states/wv.htm
Wisconsin	http://www.dpi.state.wi.us/	http://www.dpi.state.wi.us/dpi/oea/spr_kce.html
Wyoming	http://www.k12.wy.us/wdehome.html	http://www.asme.com/wycas/index.htm

Table 2 Norm-Referenced and Criterion-Referenced Tests Administered by State

STATE	NORM-REFERENCED TEST	CRITERION-REFERENCED TEST	EXIT EXAM
Alabama	Stanford Achievement Test		Alabama High School Graduation Exam
Alaska	California Achievement Test		
Arizona	Stanford Achievement Test	Arizona's Instrument to Measure Standards (AIMS)	
Arkansas	Stanford Achievement Test		
California	Stanford Achievement Test	Standardized Testing and Reporting Supplement	High School Exit Exam (HSEE)
Colorado	None	Colorado Student Assessment Program	
Connecticut		Connecticut Mastery Test	
Delaware	Stanford Achievement Test	Delaware Student Testing Program	
District of Columbia	Stanford Achievement Test		
Florida	(Locally Selected)	Florida Comprehensive Assessment Test (FCAT)	High School Competency Test (HSCT)
Georgia	Iowa Tests of Basic Skills	Criterion-Referenced Competency Tests (CRCT)	Georgia High School Graduation Tests
Hawaii	Stanford Achievement Test	Credit by Examination	Hawaii State Test of Essential Competencies
Idaho	Iowa Test of Basic Skills/ Tests of Direct Achievement and Proficiency	Writing/Mathematics Assessment	
Illinois		Illinois Standards Achievement Tests	Prairie State Achievement Examination
Indiana		Indiana Statewide Testing for Education Progress	
Iowa	(None)		
Kansas		(State-Developed Tests)	
Kentucky	Comprehensive Tests of Basic Skills	Kentucky Instructional Results Information System	
Louisiana	Iowa Tests of Basic Skills	Louisiana Educational Assessment Program	Graduate Exit Exam
Maine		Maine Educational Assessment	
Maryland		Maryland School Performance Assessment Program	
Massachusetts		Massachusetts Comprehensive Assessment System	

STATE	NORM-REFERENCED TEST	CRITERION-REFERENCED TEST	EXIT EXAM
Michigan		Michigan Educational Assessment Program	High School Test
Minnesota		Basic Standards Test	Profile of Learning
Mississippi	Iowa Test of Basic Skills	Subject Area Testing Program	Functional Literacy Examination
Missouri		Missouri Mastery and Achievement Test	
Montana	(districts' choice)		
Nebraska			
Nevada	TerraNova		Nevada High School Proficiency Examination
New Hampshire		NH Educational Improvement and Assessment Program	
New Jersey		Elementary School Proficiency Test/Early Warning Test	High School Proficiency Test
New Mexico	TerraNova		New Mexico High School Competency Exam
New York		Pupil Evaluation Program/ Preliminary Competency Test	Regents Competency Tests
North Carolina	Iowa Test of Basic Skills	NC End of Grade Test	
North Dakota	TerraNova	ND Reading, Writing Speaking, Listening, Math Test	
Ohio		Ohio Proficiency Tests	Ohio Proficiency Tests
Oklahoma	Iowa Tests of Basic Skills	Oklahoma Criterion-Referenced Tests	
Oregon		Oregon Statewide Assessment	
Pennsylvania		Pennsylvania System of School Assessment	
Rhode Island	Metropolitan Achievement Test		
South Carolina	TerraNova	Palmetto Achievement Challenge Tests	High School Exit Exam
South Dakota	Stanford Achievement Test		
Tennessee	Tennessee Comprehensive Assessment Program	Tennessee Comprehensive Assessment Program	
Texas		Texas Assessment of Academic Skills	Texas Assessment of Academic Skills
Utah	Stanford Achievement Test	Core Curriculum Testing	

STATE	NORM-REFERENCED TEST	CRITERION-REFERENCED TEST	EXIT EXAM
Vermont		New Standards Reference Exams	
Virginia	Stanford Achievement Test	Virginia Standards of Learning	Virginia Standards of Learning
Washington	Iowa Tests of Basic Skills	Washington Assessment of Student Learning	Washington Assessment of Student Learning
West Virginia	Stanford Achievement Test		
Wisconsin	TerraNova	Wisconsin Knowledge and Concepts Examinations	
Wyoming	TerraNova	Wyoming Comprehensive Assessment System	Wyoming Comprehensive Assessment System

Table 3 Standardized Test Schedules by State

STATE	KG	1	2	3	4	5	6	7	8	9	10	11	12	COMMENT
Alabama				X	X	X	X	X	X	X	X	X	X	
Alaska				X					X			X		
Arizona			X	X	X	X	X	X	X	X	X	X	X	
Arkansas					X	X		X	X		X	X	X	
California			X	X	X	X	X	X	X	X	X	X		
Colorado				X	X			X						
Connecticut					X		X		X					
Delaware				X	X	X			X		X	X		
District of Columbia		X	X	X	X	X	X	X	X	X	X	X		
Florida		X	X	X	X	X	X	X	X	X	X	X	X	There is no state-mandated norm-referenced testing. However, the state collects information furnished by local districts that elect to perform norm-referenced testing. The FCAT is administered to Grades 4, 8, and 10 to assess reading and Grades 5, 8, and 10 to assess math.
Georgia				X		X			X					
Hawaii				X			X		X		X			The Credit by Examination is voluntary and is given in Grade 8 in Algebra and Foreign Languages.
Idaho				X	X	X	X	X	X	X	X	X		
Illinois				X	X			X	X	X		X	X	Exit Exam failure will not disqualify students from graduation if all other requirements are met.
Indiana				X			X		X		X			
Iowa		*	*	*	*	*	*	*	*	*	*	*	*	*Iowa does not currently have a statewide testing program. Locally chosen assessments are administered to grades determined locally.
Kansas				X	X	X		X	X		X			

STATE	KG	1	2	3	4	5	6	7	8	9	10	11	12	COMMENT
Kentucky					X	X		X	X			X	X	
Louisiana				X		X	X	X		X				
Maine					X				X			X		
Maryland				X		X			X					
Massachusetts					X				X		X			
Michigan					X	X		X	X					
Minnesota				X		X			X					Testing Information from Fair Test.Org. There was no readily accessible state-sponsored site.
Mississippi					X	X	X	X	X					State's Web site refused connection; all data were obtained from FairTest.Org.
Missouri			X	X	X	X	X	X	X	X	X			
Montana					X				X			X		The State Board of Education has decided to use a single norm-referenced test statewide beginning 2000–2001 school year.
Nebraska		**	**	**	**	**	**	**	**	**	**	**	**	**Decisions regarding testing are left to the individual school districts.
Nevada					X				X					Districts choose whether and how to test with norm-referenced tests.
New Hampshire				X			X				X			
New Jersey				X	X			X	X	X	X	X		
New Mexico					X		X		X					
New York					X				X	X				Assessment program is going through major revisions.
North Carolina				X	X	X	X	X	X		X			NRT Testing selects samples of students, not all.
North Dakota					X		X		X		X			
Ohio					X		X			X			X	
Oklahoma				X		X		X	X		X			
Oregon				X		X			X		X			

STATE	KG	1	2	3	4	5	6	7	8	9	10	11	12	COMMENT
Pennsylvania						X	X		X	X		X		
Rhode Island				X	X	X		X	X	X	X			
South Carolina				X	X	X	X	X	X	X	X			
South Dakota			X		X	X			X	X		X		
Tennessee			X	X	X	X	X	X	X			X		
Texas				X	X	X	X	X	X		X			
Utah		X	X	X	X	X	X	X	X	X	X	X	X	
Vermont					X	X	X		X	X	X	X		Rated by FairTest.Org as a nearly model system for assessment.
Virginia				X	X	X	X		X	X		X		
Washington					X			X			X			
West Virginia		X	X	X	X	X	X	X	X	X	X	X		
Wisconsin					X				X		X			
Wyoming					X				X			X		

Testing Accommodations

The more testing procedures vary from one classroom or school to the next, the less we can compare the scores from one group to another. Consider a test in which the publisher recommends that three sections of the test be given in one 45-minute session per day on three consecutive days. School A follows those directions. To save time, School B gives all three sections of the test in one session lasting slightly more than two hours. We can't say that both schools followed the same testing procedures. Remember that the test publishers provide testing procedures so schools can administer the tests in as close a manner as possible to the way the tests were administered to the groups used to obtain test norms. When we compare students' scores to norms, we want to compare apples to apples, not apples to oranges.

Most schools justifiably resist making any changes in testing procedures. Informally, a teacher can make minor changes that don't alter the testing procedures, such as separating two students who talk with each other instead of paying attention to the test; letting Lisa, who is getting over an ear infection, sit closer to the front so she can hear better; or moving Jeffrey away from the window to prevent his looking out the window and daydreaming.

There are two groups of students who require more formal testing accommodations. One group of students is identified as having a disability under Section 504 of the Rehabilitation Act of 1973 (Public Law 93-112). These students face

some challenge but, with reasonable and appropriate accommodation, can take advantage of the same educational opportunities as other students. That is, they have a condition that requires some accommodation for them.

Just as schools must remove physical barriers to accommodate students with disabilities, they must make appropriate accommodations to remove other types of barriers to students' access to education. Marie is profoundly deaf, even with strong hearing aids. She does well in school with the aid of an interpreter, who signs her teacher's instructions to her and tells her teacher what Marie says in reply. An appropriate accommodation for Marie would be to provide the interpreter to sign test instructions to her, or to allow her to watch a videotape with an interpreter signing test instructions. Such a reasonable accommodation would not deviate from standard testing procedures and, in fact, would ensure that Marie received the same instructions as the other students.

If your child is considered disabled and has what is generally called a Section 504 Plan or individual accommodation plan (IAP), then the appropriate way to ask for testing accommodations is to ask for them in a meeting to discuss school accommodations under the plan. If your child is not already covered by such a plan, he or she won't qualify for one merely because you request testing accommodations.

The other group of students who may receive formal testing accommodations are those identified as handicapped under the Individuals with Disabilities Education Act (IDEA)—students with mental retardation, learning disabilities, serious emotional disturbance, orthopedic handicap, hearing or visual problems, and other handicaps defined in the law. These students have been identified under procedures governed by federal and sometimes state law, and their education is governed by a document called the Individualized Educational Program (IEP). Unless you are under a court order specifically revoking your educational rights on behalf of your child, you are a full member of the IEP team even if you and your child's other parent are divorced and the other parent has custody. Until recently, IEP teams actually had the prerogative to exclude certain handicapped students from taking standardized group testing altogether. However, today states make it more difficult to exclude students from testing.

If your child is classified as handicapped and has an IEP, the appropriate place to ask for testing accommodations is in an IEP team meeting. In fact, federal regulations require IEP teams to address testing accommodations. You have the right to call a meeting at any time. In that meeting, you will have the opportunity to present your case for the accommodations you believe are necessary. Be prepared for the other team members to resist making extreme accommodations unless you can present a very strong case. If your child is identified as handicapped and you believe that he or she should be provided special testing accommodations, contact the person at your child's school who is responsible for convening IEP meetings and request a meeting to discuss testing accommodations.

Problems arise when a request is made for accommodations that cause major departures from standard testing procedures. For example, Lynn has an identified learning disability in mathematics calculation and attends resource classes for math. Her disability is so severe that her IEP calls for her to use a calculator when performing all math problems. She fully under-stands math concepts, but she simply can't perform the calculations without the aid of a calculator. Now it's time for Lynn to take the school-based standardized tests, and she asks to use a calculator. In this case, since her IEP already requires her to be provided with a calculator when performing math calculations, she may be allowed a calculator during school standardized tests. However, because using a calculator constitutes a major violation of standard testing procedures, her score on all sections in which she is allowed to use a calculator will be recorded as a failure, and her results in some states will be removed from among those of other students in her school in calculating school results.

How do we determine whether a student is allowed formal accommodations in standardized school testing and what these accommodations may be? First, if your child is not already identified as either handicapped or disabled, having the child classified in either group solely to receive testing accommodations will be considered a violation of the laws governing both classifications. Second, even if your child is already classified in either group, your state's department of public instruction will provide strict guidelines for the testing accommodations schools may make. Third, even if your child is classified in either group and you are proposing testing accommodations allowed under state testing guidelines, any accommodations must still be both *reasonable* and *appropriate*. To be reasonable and appropriate, testing accommodations must relate to your child's disability and must be similar to those already in place in his or her daily educational program. If your child is always tested individually in a separate room for all tests in all subjects, then a similar practice in taking school-based standardized tests may be appropriate. But if your child has a learning disability only in mathematics calculation, requesting that all test questions be read to him or her is inappropriate because that accommodation does not relate to his identified handicap.

Glossary

Accountability The idea that a school district is held responsible for the achievement of its students. The term may also be applied to holding students responsible for a certain level of achievement in order to be promoted or to graduate.

Achievement test An assessment that measures current knowledge in one or more of the areas taught in most schools, such as reading, math, and language arts.

Aptitude test An assessment designed to predict a student's potential for learning knowledge or skills.

Content validity The extent to which a test represents the content it is designed to cover.

Criterion-referenced test A test that rates how thoroughly a student has mastered a specific skill or area of knowledge. Typically, a criterion-referenced test is subjective, and relies on someone to observe and rate student work; it doesn't allow for easy comparisons of achievement among students. Performance assessments are criterion-referenced tests. The opposite of a criterion-referenced test is a norm-referenced test.

Frequency distribution A tabulation of individual scores (or groups of scores) that shows the number of persons who obtained each score.

Generalizability The idea that the score on a test reflects what a child knows about a subject, or how well he performs the skills the test is supposed to be assessing. Generalizability requires that enough test items are administered to truly assess a student's achievement.

Grade equivalent A score on a scale developed to indicate the school grade (usually measured in months of a year) that corresponds to an average chronological age, mental age, test score, or other characteristic. A grade equivalent of 6.4 is interpreted as a score that is average for a group in the fourth month of Grade 6.

High-stakes assessment A type of standardized test that has major consequences for a student or school (such as whether a child graduates from high school or gets admitted to college).

Mean Average score of a group of scores.

Median The middle score in a set of scores ranked from smallest to largest.

National percentile Percentile score derived from the performance of a group of individuals across the nation.

Normative sample A comparison group consisting of individuals who have taken a test under standard conditions.

Norm-referenced test A standardized test that can compare scores of students in one school with a reference group (usually other students in the same grade and age, called the "norm group"). Norm-referenced tests compare the achievement of one student or the students of a school, school district, or state with the norm score.

Norms A summary of the performance of a group of individuals on which a test was standardized.

Percentile An incorrect form of the word *centile*, which is the percent of a group of scores that falls below a given score. Although the correct term is *centile*, much of the testing literature has adopted the term *percentile*.

Performance standards A level of performance on a test set by education experts.

Quartiles Points that divide the frequency distribution of scores into equal fourths.

Regression to the mean The tendency of scores in a group of scores to vary in the direction of the mean. For example: If a child has an abnormally low score on a test, she is likely to make a higher score (that is, one closer to the mean) the next time she takes the test.

Reliability The consistency with which a test measures some trait or characteristic. A measure can be reliable without being valid, but it can't be valid without being reliable.

Standard deviation A statistical measure used to describe the extent to which scores vary in a group of scores. Approximately 68 percent of scores in a group are expected to be in a range from one standard deviation below the mean to one standard deviation above the mean.

Standardized test A test that contains well-defined questions of proven validity and that produces reliable scores. Such tests are commonly paper-and-pencil exams containing multiple-choice items, true or false questions, matching exercises, or short fill-in-the-blanks items. These tests may also include performance assessment items (such as a writing sample), but assessment items cannot be completed quickly or scored reliably.

Test anxiety Anxiety that occurs in test-taking situations. Test anxiety can seriously impair individuals' ability to obtain accurate scores on a test.

Validity The extent to which a test measures the trait or characteristic it is designed to measure. Also see *reliability*.

Answer Keys for Practice Skills

Chapter 2: Word Analysis

1	D
2	C
3	B
4	A
5	B
6	C
7	B
8	D
9	D
10	B
11	B
12	A
13	C
14	B
15	B
16	B
17	A
18	C
19	C
20	B
21	C
22	C
23	D
24	A

Chapter 3: Vocabulary

1	B
2	C
3	D
4	D
5	A
6	B
7	D
8	D
9	B
10	C
11	D
12	A
13	D
14	B

Chapter 4: Reading Comprehension

1	A
2	B
3	A
4	A
5	A
6	A
7	D
8	C
9	A
10	B
11	B

Chapter 5: Listening

1	D
2	C
3	A
4	C
5	D
6	C
7	B
8	C
9	B

Chapter 6: Language Mechanics

1	B
2	B
3	C
4	A
5	D
6	A
7	A
8	A
9	A
10	A
11	C
12	D

Chapter 7: Language Expression

1	C
2	C
3	B
4	B
5	C
6	A
7	C
8	C
9	C
10	C
11	A
12	C
13	B
14	D
15	C

Chapter 8: Spelling

1	D
2	A
3	B
4	B
5	B
6	C

Chapter 9: Math Concepts

1	B
2	C
3	D
4	D
5	A
6	B
7	D
8	D
9	B
10	A
11	D
12	D
13	D
14	A
15	C
16	B
17	C

18	B
19	A
20	D
21	D
22	B
23	B
24	D
25	A
26	B
27	C
28	C
29	C
30	B
31	D
32	D

Chapter 10:
Math Computation

1	A
2	D
3	B
4	B
5	B
6	C
7	A
8	B

Chapter 11:
Math Applications

1	D
2	C
3	D
4	A
5	A
6	D
7	A
8	A
9	C
10	D
11	D
12	C
13	C
14	B
15	C
16	D
17	D
18	B
19	C
20	D
21	A
22	D
23	C
24	C
25	A
26	A

Sample Practice Test

This following sample practice test provides 250 questions organized by the skill areas presented in the preceding chapters. The sample test is intended to provide a rough idea of the types of test questions your child will probably encounter on the commercial standardized tests provided at school. It is not an exact copy.

How to Use the Test

Although it's tempting to provide guidelines to try to mimic actual testing conditions children will face in school, we chose not to do so. First, many second graders find the standardized testing procedures in school to be grueling, and we didn't wish to subject your child to a simulation that might actually increase his anxiety toward school-based standardized tests.

Second, school-based standardized tests are timed, and many children simply don't work quickly enough to finish major sections of the tests. So your child's scores on school-based standardized tests reflect both the child's mastery of the subject areas and her ability to work quickly in a timed setting. In this guide, we are more concerned with strengthening certain skills than with the ability to work under time constraints.

We don't recommend that you attempt to simulate actual testing conditions. We suggest the following alternatives for using this test:

1. Administer the test to your child after you have completed all skills chapters and have begun to implement the strategies we suggested. Allow your child to work at a leisurely pace, probably 20- to 30-minute sessions spread out over several days.

2. Administer the pertinent section of the test after you have been through each chapter and implemented the strategies.

3. Use the test as a pretest rather than as a posttest, to identify the skills on which your child needs the most work. Then concentrate most of your efforts on the skills on which your child scores the lowest.

4. Administer each section of the test before you go through each chapter as a kind of skills check to help you determine how much of your energy you need to devote to that skill area.

Administering the Test

You will need to cut out the Sample Practice Test, including the Parent Script for the Listening test. Allow your child to write in the margins as needed, such as for figuring out math problems.

Don't provide any help to your child during these tests, but note specific problems. For example, if your child has problems reading math sentences, note whether the problem is with reading rather than with math. If your child's answer sheet looks sloppy, with many erasures or cross-outs, note that you need to work on neatness. (Remember that answer sheets on tests administered at school will be machine-scored, and the scanners sometimes mistake sloppily erased answers as the answers the child intends.)

Remember to be gentle with your child during testing. If your child needs to go to the toilet or get up and get a drink, that's fine. In this test, we are more interested in gauging your child's ability in each skill area than in his ability to adhere to inflexible testing conditions.

Scoring the Test

Use the Answer Key to score your child's answers. Then enter the scores in the table below.

TEST	NUMBER CORRECT	PERCENT CORRECT	LEVEL
WORD ANALYSIS			
VOCABULARY			
READING COMPREHENSION			
LISTENING			
LANGUAGE MECHANICS			
LANGUAGE EXPRESSION			
SPELLING			
MATH CONCEPTS			
MATH COMPUTATION			
MATH APPLICATIONS			

For your convenience, here is a table to convert the number correct in each 25-question section to the percent correct:

NUMBER CORRECT	PERCENT CORRECT	NUMBER CORRECT	PERCENT CORRECT
1	4	14	56
2	8	15	60
3	12	16	64
4	16	17	68
5	20	18	72
6	24	19	76
7	28	20	80
8	32	21	84
9	36	22	88
10	40	23	92
11	44	24	96
12	48	25	100
13	52		

Interpreting the Results

As you read the following interpretations of your child's scores, remember that they are only very rough, general interpretation guidelines.

% CORRECT	INTERPRETATION
0-59	DEFINITELY NEEDS WORK
60-79	NEEDS SOME WORK
80-89	GOOD
90-100	EXCELLENT

To the Student:

These tests will give you a chance to put the tips you have learned to work. A few last reminders . . .

- Be sure you understand all the directions before you begin each test. You may ask the teacher questions about the directions if you do not understand them.

- Work as quickly as you can during each test.

- When you change an answer, be sure to erase your first mark completely.

- You can guess at an answer or skip difficult items and go back to them later.

- Use the tips you have learned whenever you can.

- It is OK to be a little nervous. You may even do better.

Now that you have completed the lessons in this book, you are on your way to scoring high!

STUDENT'S NAME

LAST — FIRST — MI

(Bubble grid A–Z for each name column)

SCHOOL

TEACHER

FEMALE ○   MALE ○

BIRTHDATE

MONTH	DAY	YEAR
JAN ○	⓪ ⓪	⓪
FEB ○	① ①	①
MAR ○	② ②	②
APR ○	③ ③	③
MAY ○	④	④
JUN ○	⑤	⑤ ⑤
JUL ○	⑥	⑥ ⑥
AUG ○	⑦	⑦ ⑦
SEP ○	⑧	⑧ ⑧
OCT ○	⑨	⑨ ⑨
NOV ○		
DEC ○		

GRADE

① ② ③ ④ ⑤ ⑥

Word Analysis

1 Ⓐ Ⓑ Ⓒ Ⓓ	6 Ⓐ Ⓑ Ⓒ Ⓓ	10 Ⓐ Ⓑ Ⓒ Ⓓ	14 Ⓐ Ⓑ Ⓒ Ⓓ	18 Ⓐ Ⓑ Ⓒ Ⓓ	22 Ⓐ Ⓑ Ⓒ Ⓓ
2 Ⓐ Ⓑ Ⓒ Ⓓ	7 Ⓐ Ⓑ Ⓒ Ⓓ	11 Ⓐ Ⓑ Ⓒ Ⓓ	15 Ⓐ Ⓑ Ⓒ Ⓓ	19 Ⓐ Ⓑ Ⓒ Ⓓ	23 Ⓐ Ⓑ Ⓒ Ⓓ
3 Ⓐ Ⓑ Ⓒ Ⓓ	8 Ⓐ Ⓑ Ⓒ Ⓓ	12 Ⓐ Ⓑ Ⓒ Ⓓ	16 Ⓐ Ⓑ Ⓒ Ⓓ	20 Ⓐ Ⓑ Ⓒ Ⓓ	24 Ⓐ Ⓑ Ⓒ Ⓓ
4 Ⓐ Ⓑ Ⓒ Ⓓ	9 Ⓐ Ⓑ Ⓒ Ⓓ	13 Ⓐ Ⓑ Ⓒ Ⓓ	17 Ⓐ Ⓑ Ⓒ Ⓓ	21 Ⓐ Ⓑ Ⓒ Ⓓ	25 Ⓐ Ⓑ Ⓒ Ⓓ
5 Ⓐ Ⓑ Ⓒ Ⓓ					

Vocabulary

1 Ⓐ Ⓑ Ⓒ Ⓓ	6 Ⓐ Ⓑ Ⓒ Ⓓ	10 Ⓐ Ⓑ Ⓒ Ⓓ	14 Ⓐ Ⓑ Ⓒ Ⓓ	18 Ⓐ Ⓑ Ⓒ Ⓓ	22 Ⓐ Ⓑ Ⓒ Ⓓ
2 Ⓐ Ⓑ Ⓒ Ⓓ	7 Ⓐ Ⓑ Ⓒ Ⓓ	11 Ⓐ Ⓑ Ⓒ Ⓓ	15 Ⓐ Ⓑ Ⓒ Ⓓ	19 Ⓐ Ⓑ Ⓒ Ⓓ	23 Ⓐ Ⓑ Ⓒ Ⓓ
3 Ⓐ Ⓑ Ⓒ Ⓓ	8 Ⓐ Ⓑ Ⓒ Ⓓ	12 Ⓐ Ⓑ Ⓒ Ⓓ	16 Ⓐ Ⓑ Ⓒ Ⓓ	20 Ⓐ Ⓑ Ⓒ Ⓓ	24 Ⓐ Ⓑ Ⓒ Ⓓ
4 Ⓐ Ⓑ Ⓒ Ⓓ	9 Ⓐ Ⓑ Ⓒ Ⓓ	13 Ⓐ Ⓑ Ⓒ Ⓓ	17 Ⓐ Ⓑ Ⓒ Ⓓ	21 Ⓐ Ⓑ Ⓒ Ⓓ	25 Ⓐ Ⓑ Ⓒ Ⓓ
5 Ⓐ Ⓑ Ⓒ Ⓓ					

Reading Comprehension

1 Ⓐ Ⓑ Ⓒ Ⓓ	6 Ⓐ Ⓑ Ⓒ Ⓓ	10 Ⓐ Ⓑ Ⓒ Ⓓ	14 Ⓐ Ⓑ Ⓒ Ⓓ	18 Ⓐ Ⓑ Ⓒ Ⓓ	22 Ⓐ Ⓑ Ⓒ Ⓓ
2 Ⓐ Ⓑ Ⓒ Ⓓ	7 Ⓐ Ⓑ Ⓒ Ⓓ	11 Ⓐ Ⓑ Ⓒ Ⓓ	15 Ⓐ Ⓑ Ⓒ Ⓓ	19 Ⓐ Ⓑ Ⓒ Ⓓ	23 Ⓐ Ⓑ Ⓒ Ⓓ
3 Ⓐ Ⓑ Ⓒ Ⓓ	8 Ⓐ Ⓑ Ⓒ Ⓓ	12 Ⓐ Ⓑ Ⓒ Ⓓ	16 Ⓐ Ⓑ Ⓒ Ⓓ	20 Ⓐ Ⓑ Ⓒ Ⓓ	24 Ⓐ Ⓑ Ⓒ Ⓓ
4 Ⓐ Ⓑ Ⓒ Ⓓ	9 Ⓐ Ⓑ Ⓒ Ⓓ	13 Ⓐ Ⓑ Ⓒ Ⓓ	17 Ⓐ Ⓑ Ⓒ Ⓓ	21 Ⓐ Ⓑ Ⓒ Ⓓ	25 Ⓐ Ⓑ Ⓒ Ⓓ
5 Ⓐ Ⓑ Ⓒ Ⓓ					

Listening

1 Ⓐ Ⓑ Ⓒ Ⓓ	6 Ⓐ Ⓑ Ⓒ Ⓓ	10 Ⓐ Ⓑ Ⓒ Ⓓ	14 Ⓐ Ⓑ Ⓒ Ⓓ	18 Ⓐ Ⓑ Ⓒ Ⓓ	22 Ⓐ Ⓑ Ⓒ Ⓓ
2 Ⓐ Ⓑ Ⓒ Ⓓ	7 Ⓐ Ⓑ Ⓒ Ⓓ	11 Ⓐ Ⓑ Ⓒ Ⓓ	15 Ⓐ Ⓑ Ⓒ Ⓓ	19 Ⓐ Ⓑ Ⓒ Ⓓ	23 Ⓐ Ⓑ Ⓒ Ⓓ
3 Ⓐ Ⓑ Ⓒ Ⓓ	8 Ⓐ Ⓑ Ⓒ Ⓓ	12 Ⓐ Ⓑ Ⓒ Ⓓ	16 Ⓐ Ⓑ Ⓒ Ⓓ	20 Ⓐ Ⓑ Ⓒ Ⓓ	24 Ⓐ Ⓑ Ⓒ Ⓓ
4 Ⓐ Ⓑ Ⓒ Ⓓ	9 Ⓐ Ⓑ Ⓒ Ⓓ	13 Ⓐ Ⓑ Ⓒ Ⓓ	17 Ⓐ Ⓑ Ⓒ Ⓓ	21 Ⓐ Ⓑ Ⓒ Ⓓ	25 Ⓐ Ⓑ Ⓒ Ⓓ
5 Ⓐ Ⓑ Ⓒ Ⓓ					

Language Mechanics

1 Ⓐ Ⓑ Ⓒ Ⓓ	6 Ⓐ Ⓑ Ⓒ Ⓓ	10 Ⓐ Ⓑ Ⓒ Ⓓ	14 Ⓐ Ⓑ Ⓒ Ⓓ	18 Ⓐ Ⓑ Ⓒ Ⓓ	22 Ⓐ Ⓑ Ⓒ Ⓓ
2 Ⓐ Ⓑ Ⓒ Ⓓ	7 Ⓐ Ⓑ Ⓒ Ⓓ	11 Ⓐ Ⓑ Ⓒ Ⓓ	15 Ⓐ Ⓑ Ⓒ Ⓓ	19 Ⓐ Ⓑ Ⓒ Ⓓ	23 Ⓐ Ⓑ Ⓒ Ⓓ
3 Ⓐ Ⓑ Ⓒ Ⓓ	8 Ⓐ Ⓑ Ⓒ Ⓓ	12 Ⓐ Ⓑ Ⓒ Ⓓ	16 Ⓐ Ⓑ Ⓒ Ⓓ	20 Ⓐ Ⓑ Ⓒ Ⓓ	24 Ⓐ Ⓑ Ⓒ Ⓓ
4 Ⓐ Ⓑ Ⓒ Ⓓ	9 Ⓐ Ⓑ Ⓒ Ⓓ	13 Ⓐ Ⓑ Ⓒ Ⓓ	17 Ⓐ Ⓑ Ⓒ Ⓓ	21 Ⓐ Ⓑ Ⓒ Ⓓ	25 Ⓐ Ⓑ Ⓒ Ⓓ
5 Ⓐ Ⓑ Ⓒ Ⓓ					

Language Expression

1 Ⓐ Ⓑ Ⓒ Ⓓ	6 Ⓐ Ⓑ Ⓒ Ⓓ	10 Ⓐ Ⓑ Ⓒ Ⓓ	14 Ⓐ Ⓑ Ⓒ Ⓓ	18 Ⓐ Ⓑ Ⓒ Ⓓ	22 Ⓐ Ⓑ Ⓒ Ⓓ
2 Ⓐ Ⓑ Ⓒ Ⓓ	7 Ⓐ Ⓑ Ⓒ Ⓓ	11 Ⓐ Ⓑ Ⓒ Ⓓ	15 Ⓐ Ⓑ Ⓒ Ⓓ	19 Ⓐ Ⓑ Ⓒ Ⓓ	23 Ⓐ Ⓑ Ⓒ Ⓓ
3 Ⓐ Ⓑ Ⓒ Ⓓ	8 Ⓐ Ⓑ Ⓒ Ⓓ	12 Ⓐ Ⓑ Ⓒ Ⓓ	16 Ⓐ Ⓑ Ⓒ Ⓓ	20 Ⓐ Ⓑ Ⓒ Ⓓ	24 Ⓐ Ⓑ Ⓒ Ⓓ
4 Ⓐ Ⓑ Ⓒ Ⓓ	9 Ⓐ Ⓑ Ⓒ Ⓓ	13 Ⓐ Ⓑ Ⓒ Ⓓ	17 Ⓐ Ⓑ Ⓒ Ⓓ	21 Ⓐ Ⓑ Ⓒ Ⓓ	25 Ⓐ Ⓑ Ⓒ Ⓓ
5 Ⓐ Ⓑ Ⓒ Ⓓ					

Spelling

1 (A)(B)(C)(D) 6 (A)(B)(C)(D) 10 (A)(B)(C)(D) 14 (A)(B)(C)(D) 18 (A)(B)(C)(D) 22 (A)(B)(C)(D)
2 (A)(B)(C)(D) 7 (A)(B)(C)(D) 11 (A)(B)(C)(D) 15 (A)(B)(C)(D) 19 (A)(B)(C)(D) 23 (A)(B)(C)(D)
3 (A)(B)(C)(D) 8 (A)(B)(C)(D) 12 (A)(B)(C)(D) 16 (A)(B)(C)(D) 20 (A)(B)(C)(D) 24 (A)(B)(C)(D)
4 (A)(B)(C)(D) 9 (A)(B)(C)(D) 13 (A)(B)(C)(D) 17 (A)(B)(C)(D) 21 (A)(B)(C)(D) 25 (A)(B)(C)(D)
5 (A)(B)(C)(D)

Math Concepts

1 (A)(B)(C)(D) 6 (A)(B)(C)(D) 10 (A)(B)(C)(D) 14 (A)(B)(C)(D) 18 (A)(B)(C)(D) 22 (A)(B)(C)(D)
2 (A)(B)(C)(D) 7 (A)(B)(C)(D) 11 (A)(B)(C)(D) 15 (A)(B)(C)(D) 19 (A)(B)(C)(D) 23 (A)(B)(C)(D)
3 (A)(B)(C)(D) 8 (A)(B)(C)(D) 12 (A)(B)(C)(D) 16 (A)(B)(C)(D) 20 (A)(B)(C)(D) 24 (A)(B)(C)(D)
4 (A)(B)(C)(D) 9 (A)(B)(C)(D) 13 (A)(B)(C)(D) 17 (A)(B)(C)(D) 21 (A)(B)(C)(D) 25 (A)(B)(C)(D)
5 (A)(B)(C)(D)

Math Computation

1 (A)(B)(C)(D) 6 (A)(B)(C)(D) 10 (A)(B)(C)(D) 14 (A)(B)(C)(D) 18 (A)(B)(C)(D) 22 (A)(B)(C)(D)
2 (A)(B)(C)(D) 7 (A)(B)(C)(D) 11 (A)(B)(C)(D) 15 (A)(B)(C)(D) 19 (A)(B)(C)(D) 23 (A)(B)(C)(D)
3 (A)(B)(C)(D) 8 (A)(B)(C)(D) 12 (A)(B)(C)(D) 16 (A)(B)(C)(D) 20 (A)(B)(C)(D) 24 (A)(B)(C)(D)
4 (A)(B)(C)(D) 9 (A)(B)(C)(D) 13 (A)(B)(C)(D) 17 (A)(B)(C)(D) 21 (A)(B)(C)(D) 25 (A)(B)(C)(D)
5 (A)(B)(C)(D)

Math Applications

1 (A)(B)(C)(D) 6 (A)(B)(C)(D) 10 (A)(B)(C)(D) 14 (A)(B)(C)(D) 18 (A)(B)(C)(D) 22 (A)(B)(C)(D)
2 (A)(B)(C)(D) 7 (A)(B)(C)(D) 11 (A)(B)(C)(D) 15 (A)(B)(C)(D) 19 (A)(B)(C)(D) 23 (A)(B)(C)(D)
3 (A)(B)(C)(D) 8 (A)(B)(C)(D) 12 (A)(B)(C)(D) 16 (A)(B)(C)(D) 20 (A)(B)(C)(D) 24 (A)(B)(C)(D)
4 (A)(B)(C)(D) 9 (A)(B)(C)(D) 13 (A)(B)(C)(D) 17 (A)(B)(C)(D) 21 (A)(B)(C)(D) 25 (A)(B)(C)(D)
5 (A)(B)(C)(D)

WORD ANALYSIS

Directions: Read the following sentences and choose the correct answer.

Example: Choose the word with the same <u>beginning</u> sound as <u>flat</u>.

   A fit

   B fig

   C floor

   D for

Answer:

   C floor

---

1 Choose the word with the same <u>beginning</u> sound as in <u>cloud</u>.

   A count

   B creep

   C crowd

   D cliff

---

2 Choose the word with the same <u>beginning</u> sound as in <u>place</u>.

   A price

   B plant

   C break

   D blank

---

3 Choose the word with the same <u>ending</u> sound as in <u>nice</u>.

   A race

   B near

   C noise

   D nose

---

4 Choose the word with the same <u>ending</u> sound as in <u>head</u>.

   A help

   B hear

   C did

   D feet

---

5 Choose the word with the same vowel sound as in <u>fuss</u>.

   A bate

   B foot

   C crust

   D face

GO

6 Choose the word with the same vowel sound as in <u>out</u>.

   A house

   B bate

   C four

   D next

7 Choose the word that has the same <u>beginning</u> consonant sound as in <u>boat</u>.

   A put

   B five

   C pout

   D bat

8 Choose the word that has the same <u>beginning</u> consonant sound as in <u>keep</u>.

   A cat

   B change

   C get

   D trap

9 Choose the word that begins with the same vowel sound as the <u>o</u> in <u>hope</u>.

   A one

   B our

   C oat

   D out

10 Choose the word that begins with the same vowel sound as <u>ee</u> in <u>keep</u>.

   A enough

   B every

   C ape

   D cape

11 Choose the word that is made up of two words.

   A enough

   B unhappy

   C tried

   D headache

12 Choose the word that is made up of two words.

   A basketball

   B beaten

   C cooked

   D aware

13 Fill in the blank: Today I wash. Yesterday I wash__.

   A ed

   B ing

   C er

   D est

14 Fill in the blank: I wanted to use the computer, but my sister was already us___ it.

A ing

B ed

C er

D able

15 Choose the word that is a contraction.

A cannot

B its

C it's

D will not

16 Choose the word that is a contraction.

A would not

B want

C does not

D don't

17 Choose the word that means would not.

A isn't

B want

C won't

D wouldn't

18 Choose the word that means the same as the contraction isn't.

A is not

B is too

C cannot

D would not

19 What is the root word or base word in the word careful?

A full

B car

C care

D are

20 What is the root word or base word in the word goodness?

A dness

B ness

C good

D goo

21 What is the suffix in the word thoughtful?

A thought

B ought

C ful

D ness

GO

22 What is the <u>suffix</u> in the word <u>fix-able</u>?

   A fix

   B able

   C xa

   D less

23 Choose the name of a number that rhymes with <u>hive</u>.

   A eleven

   B four

   C five

   D eight

24 Choose the name of a body part that rhymes with <u>south</u>.

   A ear

   B mouth

   C knee

   D chin

25 Choose the name of a color that rhymes with <u>sack</u>.

   A orange

   B red

   C blue

   D black

STOP

VOCABULARY

Directions for Questions 1 to 4: Choose the word that goes with the picture.

Example: Choose the word that goes with the picture below.

A weak

B wild

C silly

D funny

Answer:

B wild

1 A colony

B tribe

C family

D pack

2 A sorry   **B** pleased

C funny   **D** nervous

3 A crazy   **B** hungry

C angry   **D** sad

4 A regret   **B** celebration

C finished   **D** honor

Directions for Questions 5 to 8:
Read each sentence and fill in the blank.

Example: I'm having a piece of pie. Do you want _____?

   A none

   B some

   C him

   D them

Answer:

   B some

5 Angie wanted some lemonade. But when she looked in the refrigerator, she could not find ___.

   A one

   B none

   C at all

   D any

6 We wanted to cross the street, but we had to ____ until the crossing guard said we could cross.

   A run

   B go

   C wait

   D find

7 Sandra did not play very well in her first soccer game. But she played much _____ in her second game.

   A better

   B goodest

   C gooder

   D bigger

8 Sam broke his pencil. He _____ one from Janet.

   A fixed

   B sold

   C borrowed

   D threw

Directions for Questions 9 to 12: A synonym is a word that means the same as another word. Read each sentence and choose the synonym for the underlined word.

Example: The tiny baby cried out loud.

   A fat

   B hungry

   C little

   D angry

Answer:

   C little

GO

9 The <u>big</u> dog ran down the street.

   A brown

   B mean

   C brave

   D large

10 Katie stayed home from school because she was <u>sick</u>.

   A ill

   B tired

   C hungry

   D late

11 The two <u>women</u> drove into town.

   A neighbors

   B ladies

   C customers

   D drivers

12 Janice read six <u>novels</u> during her vacation.

   A magazines

   B papers

   C books

   D notes

Directions for Questions 13 to 16: An <u>antonym</u> is a word that means the <u>opposite</u> of another word. Read each sentence and choose the <u>antonym</u> for the underlined word.

Example: The boy couldn't use that toy because he was too <u>old</u>.

   A silly

   B young

   C angry

   D tall

Answer:

   B young

13 Jason did not eat the oatmeal because it was too <u>hot</u>.

   A cold

   B warm

   C sweet

   D dry

14 Look how <u>fat</u> the squirrel is.

   A brown

   B wild

   C pretty

   D thin

GO →

15 The meeting was very <u>long</u>.

  A interesting

  B dull

  C short

  D warm

16 The train whistle made a long, <u>high</u> sound.

  A loud

  B soft

  C low

  D dired

Directions for Questions 17 to 20: Read the paragraph and fill in the blank.

Example: Sally brushed her pony's mane. She was going to ride in a big horse show. She was happy. She put on the saddle and climbed onto the pony's _____.

  A head

  B nose

  C back

  D foot

Answer:

  C back

17 T. J. left the door open on his parakeet's cage. The bird flew away. T. J. was worried. But when he looked at the cage later that day, he was happy because the bird had _____.

  A flown

  B escaped

  C returned

  D sung

18 It was the first day of school. Kara looked all over for her best friend Lisa. She found Lisa sitting _____ the library.

  A instead

  B under

  C because

  D inside

19 It was very early in the morning. Fred _____ as he stretched. He was still sleepy.

  A stretched

  B sleepy

  C yawned

  D tired

GO

20 It was almost dark. Millie looked at the sky and thought, "This is the prettiest ____ I have ever seen. I see reds and blues in the sky."

A sky

B sunset

C night

D day

Directions for Questions 21 to 25: Some words have more than one meaning. Choose the word that can go into both blanks.

Example: I use a _____ for my hair. The bees put honey in their _____.

A comb   **B** rope

C brush   **D** feet

Answer:

A comb

21 Lana bought one ___ of cloth. We play out in the ___.

A yard   **B** bag

C front   **D** fence

22 I like to ___ my baby sister to sleep. I can throw a ___ all the way across the lake.

A sleep   **B** stone

C sing   **D** rock

23 My grandparents get their water from a ___. I was sick, but now I am ___.

A well   **B** healthy

C bottle **D** good

24 The elephant drank water with its ___. My mother keeps blankets in her ___.

A closet **B** nose

C trunk   **D** mouth

25 I like to ___ breakfast. My sister is a ___ at Jimbo's Restaurant.

A waitress **B** fix

C cook   **D** eat

GO

READING COMPREHENSION

Directions: Read the following story, and then answer the questions about it.

Example:

Susie was a wonderful pet owner. She always fed her cats and dogs. She played with her pets and bought them toys. Every night Susie let her pets curl up on her bed.

What is the author trying to say with this story?

A Susie is a pet doctor.

B Make Susie seem kind.

C Make Susie seem mean.

D Let you know Susie is a good mother.

Answer:

B Make Susie seem kind.

Story for Questions 1 to 4: Jane Thomas is the best person running for mayor. She taught school for 12 years and has run her own business for 7 years. She is a smart lady and a good mother.

1 What is the author trying to do in this story?

A Make you dislike Jane Thomas.

B Make you like Jane Thomas.

C Tell you how to run a business.

D Tell you why it is good to be a teacher.

---

2 Choose the sentence that tells <u>fact</u>, not <u>opinion</u>.

  A She is the best person running for mayor.

  B She taught school for 12 years.

  C She is smart.

  D She is a good mother.

---

3 What does the story NOT tell us about Jane Thomas?

  A She was a teacher.

  B She is running for mayor.

  C She has run a business.

  D She grows roses.

---

4 How long did Jane Thomas teach school?

  A 12 years   **B** 7 years   **C** 20 years   **D** She has never taught.

5 Choose the sentence that tells what is happening in this picture.

  A John swung over the creek.

  B John climbed a tree.

  C John swam across the creek.

  D John waded in the creek.

GO

Story for Questions 6 to 9: Heather's mother took her along when she voted. There were many people in line. Heather got to sit and watch cartoons with other boys and girls while her mother voted. On the way out, the lady gave Heather and her mother stickers that said, "I voted." Heather put hers on her jacket.

6 Where did Heather's mother take her?

    A to the doctor

    B to vote

    C to get her car tags

    D to the television station

7 What did Heather do while she waited for her mother?

    A She played games with other boys and girls.

    B She sat and watched cartoons.

    C She waited in the car.

    D She ate ice cream.

8 What did the lady give Heather and her mother?

    A stickers

    B ice cream

    C candy

    D their change

9 Why do you think Heather's mother had to wait a long time to vote?

    A The cartoon Heather was watching was long.

    B Her mother had to vote for many people.

    C There were many people in line.

    D Her mother had never voted before.

Story for Questions 10 to 13: The Cherokee people tell their children the legend of the little people who live among the rocks in the mountains and on the side of hills. They call them the Thunder Brothers because when you hear thunder, legend says it is the sound of the Thunder Brothers beating rocks together. The Thunder Brothers do good things such as helping lost children find their way home. If a Cherokee finds something in the woods that someone lost, such as a knife, before they take it they ask, "Thunder Brothers, may I have this?"

10 Who are the Thunder Brothers?

   A giants

   B evil spirits

   C little people

   D animals who walk and talk

11 Where do the Thunder Brothers live?

   A among the rocks

   B in villages

   C in caves

   D in teepees

12 Why do the Cherokee call these people Thunder Brothers?

   A They only come out when it thunders.

   B They make thunder sounds by beating rocks together.

   C They are afraid of thunder.

   D That is what the people told the Cherokee to call them.

13 What do the Cherokee do if they find something in the woods that someone has lost?

   A They ask the Thunder Brothers if they may keep it.

   B They leave it for the Thunder Brothers.

   C They keep it.

   D They give it to someone else.

GO

14 Choose the sentence that is make-believe.

   A   William Jefferson Clinton was elected president in 1992.

   B   Princess Palindrome flew her spaceship to the planet Zorgon.

   C   There are 50 stars on the United States flag.

   D   George Washington was the first president of the United States.

15 My name is Binky. I live in a house with my boy Don. Don pets me and takes me for walks. He gives me treats and gives me baths. I like to chase cats. What am I?

   A   a goldfish

   B   a snake

   C   a dog

   D   a turtle

Story for Questions 16 to 19: Bobby lived on a farm. He had a pet goat named Silky. Silky thought he was a dog. When Bobby would call him, Silky would come running. Bobby tried to teach Silky to fetch a ball. But when Bobby threw the ball, Silky ate it! Bobby laughed.

16 Where did Bobby live?

   A   in an apartment in town

   B   on a mountain

   C   on a boat

   D   on a farm

17 What kind of pet did Bobby have?

   A   a puppy

   B   a goat

   C   a snake

   D   a hamster

18 What was Bobby's pet's name?

    A Silky

    B Baxter

    C Biscuit

    D Chipper

19 Why did Bobby laugh?

    A His pet stood on his hind legs.

    B His pet ate the ball.

    C His pet barked out a song.

    D His pet chased a car.

Story for Questions 20 to 22: The Chieftains are musicians from Ireland. They play Irish songs. Joe went to see the Chieftains at the Peace Center. The song they played that he liked best was a jig called "Boil the Breakfast Early."

20 Where do the Chieftains come from?

    A New Jersey

    B England

    C Italy

    D Ireland

21 Where did Joe go to see The Chieftains?

    A Greenville Civic Center

    B Ireland

    C the Peace Center

    D Wolf Trap

GO

22 What is a jig?

    A   a game

    B   a fiddle

    C   a fast song that people play when they dance

    D   a flute

Story for Questions 23 to 25: Jana's parents bought a new house. It has a big backyard with a creek running through it. It has a fireplace where the family can make big fires on cold winter days. But Jana's favorite part of the house is her new room.

23 What is unusual about Jana's new backyard?

    A   It is big.

    B   There are swings in it.

    C   It has a creek running through it.

    D   It has a swimming pool.

24 What will Jana's family do on cold winter days?

    A   Go skating on the pond in the backyard.

    B   Go ice fishing down on the lake.

    C   Go skiing at Snow Mountain.

    D   Make a fire in the fireplace.

25 What is Jana's favorite part of the house?

    A   the kitchen

    B   the backyard

    C   her room

    D   the creek

PARENT SCRIPT FOR LISTENING TEST

Directions for Questions 1 to 3: Select the picture that goes with what I say.

Question 1: The girl bounced the ball on the sidewalk.

Question 2: The cat had three black feet and one white foot.

Question 3: Michael got just what he wanted for his birthday.

Story for Questions 4 to 6: Adam likes going hiking with his parents and his dog Chipper. His favorite place to go hiking is Raven's Cliff. Adam and Chipper enjoy playing at the bottom of Raven's Falls in the cold water of the Little Horse River.

Question 4: Who is Chipper?

Question 5: How do Adam and his family get to Raven's Falls?

Question 6: What do Adam and Chipper enjoy doing when they go to Raven's Cliff?

Story for Questions 7 to 9: David's big sister Bonnie is married. She has a son David's age named Paul. David and Paul enjoy riding their bicycles down to Crockett's Store where they buy Smack Cola.

Question 7: How are David and Paul related?

Question 8: How do David and Paul get to the store?

Question 9: What do David and Paul buy at the store?

Story for Questions 10 to 13: Jamie's best friend Lisa was spending the night with Jamie. Jamie's parents took them to El Paso Mexican Restaurant. Jamie likes to dip her nacho chips in the mild salsa, but Lisa likes the hot salsa. Lisa said, "Oh! I like this salsa. It is really, really hot!" Jamie laughed when she saw Lisa. "Look," Jamie said, "Lisa looks as if she is wearing lipstick."

Question 10: Who is Lisa?

Question 11: Where did Jamie's parents take Jamie and Lisa?

Question 12: Which sentence is true?

Question 13: Why did Jamie say that Lisa looked as if she was wearing lipstick?

Story for Questions 14 to 18: Johnny and Bill made a golf course in their backyard. They made a hole and tried to knock their golf balls into it. Johnny plays golf left-handed, and Bill plays right-handed. Johnny used a yellow golf ball and Bill used a green golf ball. Johnny said, "I know. Let's try something." Bill followed Johnny into the front yard. Johnny threw his golf ball over the house. Then Bill threw his golf ball over the house. When they went back to the backyard, they found Johnny's ball next to the fence, but they did not see Bill's ball. Their little sister Kelly walked by the hole they had made for their golf course. "Look!" she said as she looked into the hole.

Question 14: Who plays golf left-handed?

Question 15: Where did Johnny and Bill build a golf course?

Question 16: What did Johnny get Bill to do?

Question 17: What do you think Kelly found in the hole?

Question 18: Who is Kelly?

Story for Questions 19 to 22: Linda and Karen were identical twins. One day, they were tossing a baseball in Karen's backyard. Just as Linda tossed the ball, Karen sneezed. The ball hit her in the eye. It did not hurt much, but the next day at school, her teacher asked if she had been fighting.

Question 19: Who are Linda and Karen?

Question 20: What were they doing?

Question 21: Why did Karen not catch the ball?

Question 22: Why do you think Karen's teacher thought she had been fighting?

Story for Questions 23 to 25: Gillian was upset. She had gotten spaghetti sauce on her favorite white sweater. Her grandmother said, "Gillian, don't be upset. I can knit you another sweater. But, first, let me try something." Her grandmother went out to the garage and brought back a can of hand cleaner that Gillian's father cleaned his hands with when he worked on the truck. She rubbed some into the spaghetti stain on the sweater. She then put Gillian's sweater into a net bag and washed it on a gentle cycle in the washing machine. Gillian laughed and clapped when she took her sweater out of the washing machine. She said, "Oh, thank you, Grandmother!"

Question 23: Why was Gillian upset?

Question 24: What did Gillian's grandmother use to help solve the problem?

Question 25: Why do you think Gillian acted the way she did when she took the sweater out of the washing machine?

STOP

LISTENING

Directions to Parents: Read the descriptions on the parent script.

Tell your child: "Select the picture that goes with what I say."

1

A

B

C

D

GO

2

A

B

C

D

3

A

B

C

D

4

A Adam's dog

B Adam's father

C The Ranger at Raven's Cliff

D Adam's little brother

5

A They ride their bicycles there.

B They hike there.

C They ride a truck there.

D They get there on horses.

6

A chasing squirrels

B fishing in Little Horse River

C riding horses

D playing in the water under the falls

7

A David is Paul's cousin.

B David is Paul's uncle.

C David is Paul's brother.

D David is Paul's nephew.

8

A David's sister Bonnie takes them.

B They ride their bicycles there.

C They walk there.

D David's mother takes them.

9

A Fruit Wackies

B fresh doughnuts

C Smack Cola

D Pizza Bites

10

A Jamie's best friend

B Jamie's cousin

C Jamie's mother

D Jamie's niece

11

A to a Mexican restaurant

B to the movies

C to a 98-Degrees concert

D to watch Jamie's brother play baseball

GO

12

   A Jamie likes the hot salsa, and Lisa likes the mild salsa.

   B Jamie likes the mild salsa, and Lisa likes the hot salsa.

   C Both Jamie and Lisa like the mild salsa.

   D Both Jamie and Lisa like the hot salsa.

13

   A The hot salsa made Lisa's lips turn bright red.

   B The cherry drink that Lisa drank turned her lips bright red.

   C Lisa's lips are just more red than most people's.

   D Lisa was wearing lipstick.

14

   A Bill   **B** Kelly

   C Johnny   **D** Donna

15

   A in the park

   B in their backyard

   C in the pasture

   D on the playground at their school

16

   A Try hitting with each other's clubs.

   B Switch golf balls.

   C Throw their golf balls over the house.

   D Hit baseballs instead of golf balls.

17

   A Bill's golf ball

   B a frog

   C a ring

   D a bird's egg

18

   A Johnny and Bill's mother

   B Johnny and Bill's neighbor

   C Johnny and Bill's cousin

   D Johnny and Bill's sister

19

   A best friends

   B neighbors

   C twins

   D cousins

20

A   playing soccer

B   having a tea party

C   playing school

D   tossing a baseball

21

A   She sneezed.

B   She does not catch well.

C   She was not wearing her glasses.

D   Someone called her name.

22

A   Some other children said she had been fighting.

B   She had a black eye.

C   She and Linda were angry with each other.

D   She had a bandage wrapped around her hand.

23

A   She had gotten a stain on her favorite sweater.

B   Her grandmother was going home soon.

C   She tore a hole in her favorite sweater.

D   She did not like spaghetti.

24

A   hand cleaner

B   hairspray

C   spot remover

D   toothpaste

25

A   Her grandmother knitted her a new sweater.

B   She enjoyed using the washing machine.

C   The stain was gone.

D   Her sweater smelled very nice.

STOP

LANGUAGE MECHANICS

Directions for Questions 1 to 9:
These sentences are divided into four parts each, lettered A to D. Choose the part that has a word that should be capitalized but is not.

Example:

    A   Susie and Jim

    B   went to france

    C   on a vacation

    D   with their family.

Answer:

    B   went to <u>f</u>rance (France)

---

1 **A**   Baxter and sparky

    B   are puppies

    C   who live

    D   on Oak Street.

---

2 **A**   When Rosa goes to

    B   sally's house,

    C   they jump

    D   on Sally's trampoline.

---

3 **A**   Gerald's

    B   best friend

    C   bart has a little

    D   sister named Kelli.

---

4 **A**   Jim and David

    B   went to see Wallop the Clown

    C   at the

    D   smith Auditorium.

---

5 **A**   Oak street

    B   is two

    C   streets west

    D   from South Avenue.

---

6 **A**   Karen and

    B   Sarah rode

    C   their bicycles

    D   to crandall's store.

---

7 **A**   We hiked

    B   all day

    C   to reach

    D   Cold mountain.

---

8 **A**   We start

    B   school in August

    C   and get out

    D   in june.

9 A when Tana

  B and Kelly

  C visit Lisa,

  D they have lots of fun.

Directions for Questions 10 to 18:
Choose the sentence with correct punctuation.

Example:

  A Are you going to the party!

  B Look out!

  C Let's go to the beach?

  D Where are the dishes

Answer:

  B Look out!

10 A Heather is six, years old.

  B Where does Bill live!

  C Why did you do that.

  D I went to the store yesterday.

11 A Did you see the movie!

  B Wow! What a movie!

  C Wow? What a movie?

  D We all yelled "Surprise?" at the same time.

12 A Janet likes peaches and, Faye, likes cherries.

  B Janet, likes peaches and Faye, likes cherries.

  C Janet, do you prefer peaches or cherries!

  D Janet likes peaches, and Faye likes cherries.

13 A Jeffrey likes wrestling. Adam likes football.

  B Jeffrey likes wrestling, Adam likes football.

  C Jeffrey, likes wrestling. Adam, likes football.

  D Jeffrey! likes wrestling. Adam! likes football.

14 A I have never seen such a beautiful sunset!

  B Have you ever seen such a beautiful sunset!

  C What time is sunset on Tuesday!

  D What time is sunset on Tuesday.

GO ⇨

15 **A** He brought tea juice, and water to drink.

B He, brought tea, juice, and water to drink.

C He brought tea, juice, and water to drink.

D He. Brought tea, juice, and water to drink.

16 **A** Goodnight Uncle Jim have a good night's sleep.

B Goodnight Uncle Jim, have a good night's sleep.

C Goodnight, Uncle Jim. Have a good night's sleep.

D Goodnight. Uncle Jim. Have a good night's sleep.

17 **A** He, picked apples pears and peaches in his backyard.

B He picked apples pears and peaches in his backyard.

C He picked apples, pears, and peaches in his backyard.

D He picked apples pears, and peaches in his backyard.

18 **A** We went to Marys birthday party.

B We, went to Mary's. Birthday party.

C We went to Mary's birthday party.

D We went, to Marys, birthday party.

Directions for Questions 19 to 25: Choose the sentence with correct capitalization and punctuation.

Example:

A Fiona and kate ran, down the street.

B fiona and Kate ran down the street.

C Fiona and Kate ran down the street.

D Fiona, and Kate, ran down the street.

Answer:

C Fiona and Kate ran down the street.

GO

19
  A   Baxter Biscuit and Sparky chased fluffy down oak street.

  B   Baxter, Biscuit, and Sparky chased Fluffy down Oak Street.

  C   Baxter, biscuit, and sparky chased fluffy down oak street.

  D   Baxter. Biscuit. And Sparky chased Fluffy down Oak Street.

20
  A   Boy! That was good!

  B   Boy! that was good!

  C   Boy. That was good.

  D   Hi, my name is bigfoot.

21
  A   Charlie is left-handed, But Sam is right-handed.

  B   Charlie is left-handed, but Sam is right-handed.

  C   Charlie is Left-Handed, but Sam is Right-Handed.

  D   Charlie is left-handed but sam is right-handed.

22
  A   One dollar is good, and two dollars are better, but three dollars are best.

  B   One dollar, is good. and two dollars are better. but three dollars are best,

  C   One $dollar is good, and two $dollars are better, but three $dollars are best.

  D   One dollar is good and two dollars are better but three dollars are best.

23
  A   How did Peta know which door to open?

  B   How did Peta know which door to open.

  C   How, did Peta know which door to open?

  D   How! Did Peta know which door to open!

24
  A   Jamie asked where did Chip go.

  B   Jamie asked, "Where did Chip go?"

  C   Jamie asked where did Chip go?

  D   Jamie asked, "Where did Chip go"?

25
  A   Bill, said, "To turn left."

  B   Bill said to turn left.

  C   Bill said, "To turn left."

  D   Bill. Said, "To turn left."

STOP

LANGUAGE EXPRESSION

Directions for Questions 1 to 16: Choose the correct word to go in each blank.

Example: Two _____ were grazing in the field.

  A pony's

  B ponys

  C ponys'

  D ponies

Answer:

  D ponies

1 Both ____ were wearing black dresses.

  A womans

  B wemen

  C women

  D womanses

2 I just saw two ___ swim by.

  A fishes

  B fish's

  C fish

  D fesh

3 One balloon is good, but two ___ are better.

  A balloonses

  B balleen

  C balloons

  D balloonz

4 I went to two birthday ___ on Saturday.

  A parties

  B partys

  C partyes

  D parteys

5 ___ looked for his socks.

  A Him

  B His

  C He

  D Her

6 Sarah went to visit ___ grand-mother.

  A her

  B she

  C them

  D hers

GO

7 Angela wanted to ride her bicycle, but ___ had a flat tire.

A he

B it

C they

D her

8 Sam and Ted live in the country. ___ ride a bus to school.

A He

B Them

C Their

D They

9 Did Sela __ to the store today?

A goes

B goed

C went

D go

10 Where did Adam ___ the book?

A bought

B buyed

C brought

D buy

11 Michael ___ me where to find my key.

A tells

B telled

C told

D telling

12 The bird ___ away from the tree.

A flied

B flew

C fly

D flown

13 One ice cream cone is good, two ice cream cones are ___, but three ice cream cones are best.

A good

B better

D bester

D gooder

14 The baseball is small, the golf ball is smaller, and the ping pong ball is ____.

A smalling

B smallest

C smaller

D small

GO

15 That boy is the ____ boy I have ever met.

   A brave

   B braver

   C braved

   D bravest

16 When you wash the sweater, use the ___ amount of soap powder that you can.

   A little

   B less

   C lesser

   D least

Directions for Questions 17 to 19: Choose the sentence that makes sense.

Example:

   A Did you hear that, listen?

   B Listen, did you hear that?

   C That, listen did you hear?

   D You, listen hear that?

Answer:

   B Listen, did you hear that?

17 **A** Cookie Paul did eat the last?

   B Did Paul the cookie last eat

   C Did Paul eat the last cookie?

   D Cookie did pall the eat last?

18 **A** Jarrod said, "Let I tell you."

   B Jarrod said, "Tell you I let."

   C Jarrod said, "Let me tell you."

   D Let Jarrod I tell you me said.

19 **A** I cannot put up with that noise.

   B Up with that noise I cannot put.

   C Noise up with that put up with I cannot.

   D Noise up with that I cannot put.

Directions for Questions 20 to 22: Choose the sentence that is written INCORRECTLY.

Example:

   A I ain't got no pie.

   B There is no pie.

   C Do you have any pie?

   D I don't have any pie.

Answer:

   A I ain't got no pie.

20 **A** I never saw no eagle.

   B I never saw an eagle.

   C I never saw any eagles.

   D I wanted to see an eagle.

21 **A** Diane did not go anywhere.

  B Diane went nowhere.

  C Diane will not go anywhere.

  D Diane did not go nowhere.

22 **A** Ginger did not pay him nothing for the apples.

  B Ginger did not pay him anything for the apples.

  C Ginger paid him nothing for the apples.

  D Did Ginger pay him anything for the apples?

Directions for Questions 23 to 25: Choose the correct sentence to end the paragraph.

Example: Kara likes to write stories. First she sits down at her desk. She gathers her pens and paper. She likes to listen to the radio while she writes.

  A When she's finished writing, Kara draws pictures to go with the story.

  B Kara lives with her aunt and uncle in California.

  C Sam's favorite food is fish sticks.

  D Adam likes to play with his puppy.

Answer:

  A When she's finished writing, Kara draws pictures to go with the story.

23 Joe has a parakeet named Pat. Pat lives in a nice cage. Joe feeds Pat bird seed.

  A Jamie has an aunt named Pat.

  B Pat likes the big seeds better than the little seeds.

  C Michael pats his foot when he hears music.

  D Theresa has a pet lizard.

24 Tom makes copies of animal tracks. First he finds a nice track. Then he pours wet plaster into the track.

  A Tom's brother is named David.

  B Tom was named after his father.

  C Bears make bigger tracks than dogs.

  D When the plaster gets hard, Tom digs it out of the ground.

25 Carol has a new computer. She got a printer with it.

  A My grandmother has never used a computer.

  B Carol makes better grades in math than she does in English.

  C She likes to write stories on it.

  D Carol is right-handed, but Joe is left-handed.

SPELLING

Directions for Questions 1 to 19:
Read the sentence and choose the correct word to go in the blank.

Example: I _____ a song with the chorus.

   A   singed

   B   sung

   C   singing

   D   sang

Answer:

   D   sang

1 The rabbit ____ down the hill.

   A   hoped

   B   hoppeted

   C   hopped

   D   hop

2 The ___ were falling off the tree.

   A   leafs

   B   leves

   C   leefs

   D   leaves

3 I ___ a letter to my cousin T. J.

   A   rote

   B   wrote

   C   rited

   D   writ

4 We made a ___ of lemonade.

   A   jug

   B   joog

   C   jhug

   D   juge

5 Two plus six is ____.

   A   eight

   B   ate

   C   eat

   D   aight

6 I will ___ Aunt Grace a thank you note for the present.

   A   write

   B   right

   C   wright

   D   rite

GO

7 Two ___ were sitting on the bench.

A wemen

B womans

C women

D wimin

8 The dog ___ on the front steps.

A sleeped

B slepd

C slepped

D slept

9 I went to my friend's house, and we ___ in his front yard.

A plaid

B played

C pleyd

D plaad

10 Kyle ___ her new bicycle down the street.

A road

B rided

C rode

D rid

11 John ___ his dog's house green.

A painted

B panted

C pented

D pinted

12 A butterfly landed on Bill's ___.

A noz

B nose

C noaz

D noze

13 Lynn ___ off the swing.

A fell

B feel

C falled

D fallen

14 John's __ are brown, but his sister's are green.

A ize

B eas

C ise

D eyes

GO

15 When Tom fell down, he skinned his ___.

A nee   **B** knee

C nea   **D** ni

---

16 Do you ___ well today?

A feel   **B** file

C fele   **D** feal

---

17 Will you ___ me how to tie my karate belt?

A sho   **B** show

C shoaw   **D** showe

---

18 Did she ___ Jeff how to ride his bicycle?

A teech   **B** teche

C teetch   **D** teach

---

19 ___ pass the butter.

A Please   **B** Pleese

C Plese   **D** Pleeze

Directions for Questions 20 to 25: Look at the underlined words. Which one is NOT spelled correctly?

20 Henry <u>ran</u> <u>down</u> the <u>street</u> with his
             A   **B**   **C**

<u>dogg</u>.
D

---

21 Shannon did not <u>feal</u> <u>well</u>, so she
                   A   **B**

<u>called</u> her mother to <u>come</u> get her.
C   **D**

---

22 Anna <u>has</u> a bad <u>cold</u> and has to <u>blo</u>
         A   **B**   **C**

her <u>nose</u> a lot.
     D

---

23 Jana <u>missed</u> the ball the <u>first</u> time,
       A   **B**

but she <u>tride</u> much <u>harder</u> the next
         C   **D**

time and hit the ball.

---

24 Bob <u>threw</u> the <u>ball</u> to Ross, and he
       A   **B**

<u>throo</u> it <u>back</u>.
C   **D**

---

25 Please <u>luk</u> both <u>ways</u> before you
       A   **B**

<u>cross</u> the <u>road</u>.
C   **D**

STOP

MATH CONCEPTS

Directions: Read the following questions and choose the right answer.

Example: What word goes in the blank?

Seventy, eighty, _____, one hundred

A nineteen

B nineteeny

C ninety

D ninty

Answer:

C ninety

---

1 What word goes in the blank?

twenty, thirty, forty, ___, sixty

A fifty

B fivety

C fifeteen

D fivty

---

2 Choose the number that is <u>more than</u> any of these numbers: 32, 18, 27, 51

A 14

B 23

C 45

D 67

---

3 Choose the numbers that are in the correct order from smallest to largest.

A 39, 40, 57, 23

B 13, 27, 39, 45

C 67, 53, 49, 32

D 18, 67, 23, 49

---

4 We are going to count by tens. Fill in the missing number: 10, 20, ___, 40, 50

A 50

B 40

C 30

D 100

GO

5 What place is the girl in line for tickets?

    A third   **B** fourth   **C** fifth   **D** second

6 About how many inches tall is the mouse?

    A 6   **B** 10   **C** 4   **D** 2

7 How much of the pizza has been removed?

    A one-half   **B** one-eighth   **C** seven-eighths   **D** one-fourth

8 Choose the one that is NOT a real number sentence.

    A $3 + 6 = 9$ **B** $6 - 3 = 3$ **C** $3 \& 6) 12$ **D** $2 = 3 - 1$

9 Choose the number that stands for 8 tens and 6 ones.

    A 68   **B** 86   **C** 860   **D** 680

10 Choose the number that stands for 4 hundreds, 6 tens, and 4 ones.

    A 400604   **B** 4064   **C** 464   **D** 446

GO

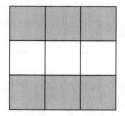

11 Choose the pattern with the blocks missing from this pattern.

A 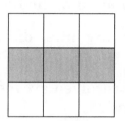 **B** 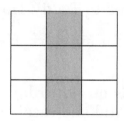 **C** 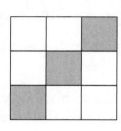 **D**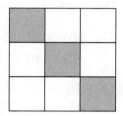

12 Figure out the pattern in these numbers and then fill in the blank: 1, 3, 5, 7, __.

   A 8   **B** 9   **C** 6   **D** 12

13 John bought $3.23 worth of candy. He only has dollar bills, no pennies, nickels, dimes, or quarters. How many one-dollar bills must he give the cashier to pay for the candy?

   A 5   **B** 4   **C** 3   **D** 6

14 We want to put the numbers in the correct order from smallest to largest. Choose the number that should go in the blank: 17, 23, __, 37, 49

   A 14   **B** 43   **C** 29   **D** 59

15 We are going to count by threes. Fill in the blank: 3, 6, 9, __, 15, 18

   A 10   **B** 11   **C** 12   **D** 14

16 Choose the number sentence that is true.

   A 6 + 4 = 9   **B** 9 − 4 = 5   **C** 5 + 5 = 55   **D** 8 − 5 = 13

GO

17 The number is 869. What number is in the tens place?

    A 8   **B** 6   **C** 9   **D** 4

---

18 Choose the problem that we would solve by using <u>subtraction</u>.

    A The train had 27 cars. Three more were added in Springfield. How many cars did it have then?

    B Jana had eight books. She gave three to Teddy. How many did she have left?

    C Russell walked two miles each day for six days. How many miles did he walk in all?

    D Janice received three birthday cards on Saturday. She received six more on Monday. How many birthday cards did she receive in all?

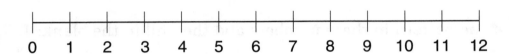

19 If you start at 11 and move 6 spaces to the left and circle the number, which number will you circle?

    A 3   **B** 4   **C** 6   **D** 5

---

20 Choose the sentence that means "5 is greater than 3."

    A $5 > 3$ **B** $5 < 3$ **C** $5 - 3$ **D** $5 + 3$

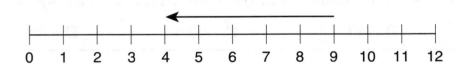

21 If you start at 9 and end at 4, how many spaces to the left do you have to move?

    A 9   **B** 6   **C** 4   **D** 5

GO

22 In which group are both numbers under the triangles larger than both numbers under the squares?

A

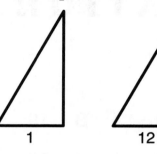

1   12

5   10

B

9   3

6   9

C

5   9

1   3

D

6   8

7   9

23

100s	10s	1s

A 457   B 574   C 475   D 447

---

24 What numeral is between 49 and 63?

A 61   B 27   C 64   D 19

---

25 Choose the symbol that we need to make this number sentence true.
18 __ 11 = 7

A >   B <   C +   D −

STOP

MATH COMPUTATION

Directions: Solve each problem.

Example:

```
  2
+2
```

A 2   **B** 4

C 0   **D** 5

Answer:

B 4

1
```
  23
+23
```

A 64   **B** 23

C 46   **D** 32

2
```
  19
−12
```

A 7   **B** 8

C 21   **D** 12

3
```
  9
+9
```

A 18   **B** 19

C 20   **D** 29

4
```
  9
−7
```

A 12   **B** 6

C 2   **D** 9

---

5 $15 - \underline{\quad} = 7$

A 9   **B** 6

C 5   **D** 8

---

6 $5 + 7 = \underline{\quad}$

A 9   **B** 12

C 15   **D** 13

7
```
  3
  2
+7
```

A 13   **B** 12

C 9   **D** 11

GO →

8 $12 - 3 + 2 =$ __

A 23   **B** 19

C 11   **D** 9

---

9 15
-7
$+2$

A 21   **B** 12

C 3   **D** 10

---

10 $ 3.12
$+ 1.89$

A $4.01   **B** $5.01

C $4.91   **D** $5.11

---

11 __ $+ 6 = 14$

A 4   **B** 10

C 8   **D** 7

---

12 $7 + 8 + 3 =$ __

A 20   **B** 8

C 18   **D** 15

---

13   23¢
$+19$¢

A 39¢   **B** 57¢

C 39¢   **D** 42¢

---

14   669
-336

A 926   **B** 303

C 237   **D** 333

---

15 $219 - 107 =$ ___

A 419   **B** 106

C 123   **D** 112

---

16 $5 - 3 =$ __

A 2   **B** 8

C 4   **D** 11

---

17 $9.67
-5.25

A $442.00   **B** $4.42

C $44.20   **D** $0.42

GO

18   33
     33
  +33

    A 66   **B** 99

    C 100   **D** 89

19 16
   −4
  +4

    A 12   **B** 20

    C 16   **D** 24

20   19
  +12

    A 21   **B** 41

    C 12   **D** 31

21 $19 - \underline{} = 7$

    A 11   **B** 12

    C 5   **D** 10

22   41
  −13

    A 18   **B** 48

    C 38   **D** 28

23 $0.23
  +0.88

    A $1.01   **B** $1.11

    C $1.21   **D** $1.31

24 $25 - \underline{} = 7$

    A 8   **B** 18

    C 28   **D** 7

25   222
  +444

    A 999   **B** 566

    C 606   **D** 666

STOP

MATH APPLICATIONS

1 Choose the picture of the object that you think weighs about the same as the bowling ball.

A    **B**    **C**    **D**

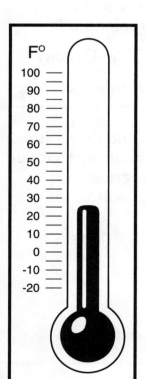

2 Choose the picture that shows what Sam and Jane would be doing when it is this temperature outside.

A    **B**

C    **D**

163

3 Find the perimeter of this square.

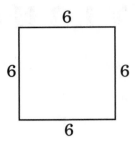

A 12   **B** 18

C 30   **D** 24

---

4 Choose the number sentence that will solve this problem: Rick paid $3.12 for books, $2.15 for a notebook, and $4.19 for stickers. If the cashier added 48 cents tax, how much did Rick pay in all?

A $3.12 + $2.15 = ___

B $3.12 – $2.15 – $.48 = ___

C $3.12 + $.48 = ___

D $3.12 + $2.15 + $4.19 + $.48 = ___

---

5 Choose the one that is the shape of a cone.

A   **B**

C   **D**

Directions: Use this calendar to answer Questions 6 and 7.

September

Sunday	Monday	Tuesday	Wednesday	Thursday	Friday	Saturday
	1	2	3	4	5	6
7	(8)	9	10	11	12	13
14	15	16	17	18	19	20
21	22	23	24	25	26	27
28	29	30				

6 Elaine's birthday is September 8. What day of the week will her birthday be on this calendar?

A Monday   **B** Wednesday

C Friday   **D** Sunday

---

7 On September 22, Linda's mother told her, "Linda, remember that you have your dance program next Monday." What date will Linda's dance program be?

A September 29

B September 23

C September 18

D September 30

8 What shape has five sides?

A triangle

B parallelogram

C oval

D pentagon

9 Choose the one that is a sphere.

A
B

C
D

10 What is the total value of these coins?

A 35¢

B 42¢

C $1.00

D 50¢

11 Michael had four cookies. He decided to share half of them with his friend Susan. How many cookies did he give Susan?

A 4   **B** 2

C 8   **D** 1

12 What time is shown on this clock?

A 5:20

B 4:25

C 6:15

D 5:30

13 Which figure's two sides will NOT match when the figure is folded along the dotted lines?

A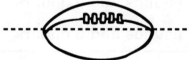

B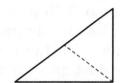

C

D

GO

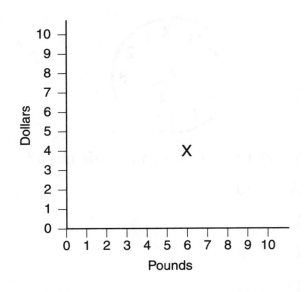

14 What value does the <u>X</u> mark?

A   6 pounds and 4 dollars

B   2 pounds and 10 dollars

C   5 pounds and 5 dollars

D   4 pounds and 6 dollars

15 Joshua left home at 3:15 p.m. to play with Carl. His mother said, "Joshua, be home in an hour and a half." When was Joshua supposed to return home?

A   3:45 p.m.   **B**   5:45 p.m.

C   5:15 p.m.   **D**   4:45 p.m.

16 Jane had three red marbles and two blue marbles in a bag. She reached in and, without looking, took a marble. What is the chance that she took a blue marble?

A   2 out of 5   **B**   3 out of 5

C   3 out of 2   **D**   2 out of 2

17 Choose the sentence that is true.

A   The boy is on the horse.

B   The boy is behind the horse.

C   The boy is under the horse.

D   The boy is beside the horse.

Directions for Questions 18 and 19: Look at the graph of the number of books read by the children in four classes. Answer the following questions using the graph.

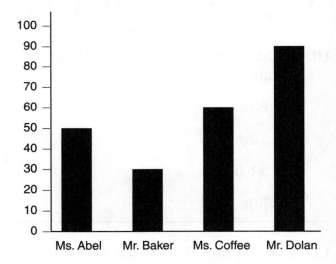

18 How many books did Ms. Coffee's class read?

A   60   **B**   90

C   50   **D**   30

19 Which teacher's class read the least number of books?

A Ms. Abel

B Mr. Baker

C Ms. Coffee

D Mr. Dolan

20 Coach Smith timed how long each player took to run from one basketball goal to the basketball goal on the other side of the gym. When she wrote down each player's time, she wrote down the number of ____ each player took.

A weeks

B seconds

C hours

D days

21 How many books wide is the book bag?

A 10   **B** 3

C 6   **D** 15

22 Angela wanted to see how far she could kick a soccer ball. She put her cap down next to where she would put the ball to kick it. Her brother Jason stood where the ball landed when Angela kicked it. What two units of measurement could Angela use to measure how far she kicked the soccer ball?

A feet or grams

B meters or liters

C feet or meters

D grams or liters

Directions for Questions 23 to 25: Here is a table of the number of children in four teachers' classes:

	Ms. Acker	Mr. Black	Ms. Carson	Mr. Dugan
Boys	8	11	6	9
Girls	11	9	12	10
Total	19	20	18	19

23 Whose class has the most boys?

A Ms. Acker

B Ms. Carson

C Mr. Black

D Mr. Dugan

24 Whose class has the fewest students in all?

A Mr. Acker

B Ms. Carson

C Mr. Black

D Mr. Dugan

25 Which two teachers' classes have the same number of students?

A Ms. Acker and Ms. Carson

B Mr. Black and Mr. Dugan

C Ms. Acker and Mr. Dugan

D Mr. Dugan and Ms. Carson

STOP

Answer Key for Sample Practice Test

Word Analysis

1	D
2	B
3	A
4	C
5	C
6	A
7	D
8	A
9	C
10	A
11	D
12	A
13	A
14	A
15	C
16	D
17	D
18	A
19	C
20	C
21	C
22	B
23	C
24	B
25	D

Vocabulary

1	C
2	C
3	C
4	B
5	D
6	C
7	A
8	C
9	D
10	A
11	B
12	C
13	A
14	D
15	C
16	C
17	C
18	D
19	C
20	B
21	A
22	D
23	A
24	C
25	C

Reading Comprehension

1	B
2	B
3	D
4	A
5	D
6	B
7	B
8	A
9	C
10	C
11	A
12	B
13	A
14	B
15	C
16	D
17	B
18	A
19	B
20	D
21	C
22	C
23	C
24	D
25	C

Listening

1	D
2	A
3	C
4	A
5	B
6	D
7	B
8	B
9	C
10	A
11	A
12	B
13	A
14	C
15	B
16	C

17	A
18	D
19	C
20	D
21	A
22	B
23	A
24	A
25	C

Language Mechanics

1	A
2	B
3	C
4	D
5	A
6	D
7	D
8	D
9	A
10	D
11	B
12	D
13	A
14	A
15	C
16	C
17	C
18	C
19	B
20	A
21	B
22	A

23	A
24	B
25	B

Language Expression

1	C
2	C
3	C
4	A
5	C
6	A
7	B
8	D
9	D
10	D
11	C
12	B
13	B
14	B
15	D
16	D
17	C
18	C
19	A
20	A
21	D
22	A
23	B
24	D
25	C

Spelling

1	C
2	D
3	B

4	A
5	A
6	A
7	C
8	D
9	B
10	C
11	A
12	B
13	A
14	D
15	B
16	A
17	B
18	D
19	A
20	D
21	A
22	C
23	C
24	C
25	A

Math Concepts

1	A
2	D
3	B
4	C
5	B
6	C
7	B
8	C
9	B
10	C
11	A

12	B
13	B
14	C
15	C
16	B
17	B
18	B
19	D
20	A
21	D
22	C
23	A
24	A
25	D

Math Computation

1	C
2	A
3	A
4	C
5	D
6	B
7	B
8	C
9	D
10	B
11	C
12	C
13	D
14	D
15	D
16	A
17	B
18	B
19	C

20	D
21	B
22	D
23	B
24	B
25	D

Math Applications

1	D
2	C
3	D
4	D
5	B
6	A
7	A
8	D
9	B
10	D
11	B
12	A
13	B
14	A
15	D
16	A
17	D
18	A
19	B
20	B
21	C
22	C
23	C
24	B
25	C

WORKSHEET

WORKSHEET

WORKSHEET